SCYTHIANS

R. Jaxartes

MASSAGETES

SOGDIANA

• Alexandria Eschata

• Alexandria Oxiana

R. Oxus

BACTRIA

GANDHARA

Bactra •

• Taxila

Caspian Sea

COLCHIS

IBERIA

ALBANIA

• Artaxata

Trapezus

ARMENIA

Alexandria Arion •   • Alexandria (Herat)

ARACHOSIA

• Alexandria Sogdia

ATROPATENE

DRANGIANA

R. Indus

Nisibis •   Gaugamela •

MEDIA

• Alexandria (Kandahar)

Edessa •

• Arbela

• Carrhae   Hatra •

• Ecbatana

ASSYRIA

R. Tigris

SUSIANA

PERSIS

Pattala •

R. Euphrates

Ctesiphon •

• Susa

• Alexandria Portus (Karach

...YRIA

BABYLONIA

• Babylon

Pasargadae •

• Palmyra

• Persepolis

...olis

Baalbek •

Damascus •

...n

...rea

...alem

ARABIANS

...tra

NABATAEANS

The Classical World

	Sea level (or below) to 200 metres
	200 metres – 500 metres
	500 metres – 1000 metres
	1000 metres – 3000 metres
–·–·–	Eastern boundary of Alexander's conquest
– – –	Eastern frontier of Roman Empire

Felsina (Bologna) •   • Spina

Marzabotto •

Faesulae (Fiesole) •

Volaterrae (Volterra) •   Arretium (Arezzo) •

Clusium (Chiusi) •   • Perusia (Perugia)

Populonia •   • Vetulonia

Volsinii (Bolsena) •

Vulci •

ETRURIA

• Falerii (Civita Castellana)

Tarquinii (Tarquinia) •

Pyrgi • Caere • Veii

• Praeneste

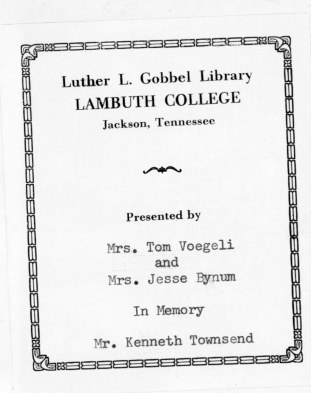
The subjects illustrated on this jacket are
FRONT: *The Piombino Apollo*, Louvre, Paris.
Photograph Michael Holford. BACK: *The
Arch of Titus*, Rome. Photograph Kersting.

The Classical World

THE CLASSICAL WORLD

DONALD E. STRONG

Assistant Keeper, Department of Greek and Roman Antiquities,
British Museum, London

McGRAW-HILL BOOK COMPANY
NEW YORK · TORONTO

General Editors

BERNARD S. MYERS   TREWIN COPPLESTONE
New York   *London*

PREHISTORIC AND PRIMITIVE MAN
Dr Andreas Lommel, Director of the Museum of Ethnology, Munich

THE ANCIENT WORLD
Professor Giovanni Garbini, Institute of Near Eastern Studies, University of Rome

THE CLASSICAL WORLD
Dr Donald Strong, Assistant Keeper, Department of Greek and Roman Antiquities, British Museum, London

THE EARLY CHRISTIAN AND BYZANTINE WORLD
Professor Jean Lassus, Institute of Art and Archaeology, University of Paris

THE WORLD OF ISLAM
Dr Ernst J. Grube, Associate Curator in Charge, Islamic Department, Metropolitan Museum of Art, New York

THE ORIENTAL WORLD
Jeannine Auboyer, Keeper at the Musée Guimet, Paris
Dr Roger Goepper, Director of the Department of Oriental Art, State Museums, Berlin

THE MEDIEVAL WORLD
Peter Kidson, Conway Librarian, Courtauld Institute of Art, London

MAN AND THE RENAISSANCE
Andrew Martindale, Senior Lecturer in the School of Fine Arts, University of East Anglia

THE AGE OF BAROQUE
Michael Kitson, Lecturer in the History of Art, Courtauld Institute of Art, London

THE MODERN WORLD
Norbert Lynton, Head of the School of Art History and General Studies, Chelsea School of Art, London

Library of Congress Catalog Card Number 65-21594
62234

© PAUL HAMLYN LIMITED 1965

PRINTED IN THE NETHERLANDS BY JOH. ENSCHEDÉ EN ZONEN
GRAFISCHE INRICHTING N.V. · HAARLEM

List of Contents

Colour Plates

Head of Apollo, Olympia Museum, Greece

Introduction

It takes less effort of the imagination to picture a Greek statue, or a Greek temple, than works of art of any other period, and the very familiarity of these things makes it difficult to appreciate the magnitude of the Greek achievement. We need to remind ourselves constantly that it was the Greeks who discovered the methods of representing man and nature in sculpture and painting which we accept as natural, and that very often when we observe in the history of Greek art some vital step towards the understanding of the human body, of the rules of perspective, of modelling in colour and so on, we are observing something which is happening for the first time.

THE SCOPE AND PURPOSE OF THIS BOOK

'Classical' is a word that has many meanings. In the title of this book it means, broadly speaking, Greek and Roman, one of its most widely accepted senses. But when we speak of 'Classical' art we mean much more than the artistic output of the Greeks and Romans. We imply an ideal. The Greeks of the 5th century believed that the highest aspirations of the spirit could be expressed in a perfection of human form based upon harmony and proportion; that perfect humanity implies the perfection of a universal order. The classical spirit and the classical tradition in art survived as long as something of this ideal, this fundamental belief in humanity, remained the source of inspiration, and all subsequent classical revivals have tried to recapture it.

This book is concerned with a very long period of time; three thousand years from the 3rd millennium BC to the 4th century AD. Its theme is the origin and development of Greek art and the spread of the Greek tradition. Every part of this long period has its own contribution to make. There are of course periods when the creative stimulus was strongest, but, from the point of view of western art and indeed of western civilisation, the whole development of the classical tradition from its beginnings right through to late Roman times is of vital importance to us. This book ends in the 4th century AD, not because the classical tradition was dead but because the Christian faith, while continuing to draw inspiration from pagan artistic traditions, introduced into art fundamentally different conceptions of truth and beauty.

This book aims to provide an outline account of classical art in terms of the history of the time and, by explaining the circumstances in which the art was produced, give a basis for understanding it. A history of art need not, and probably had better not, attempt to pass judgement upon it. Nor does it offer objective standards of judgement. It can, however, discourage false standards by stressing the different aims and ideals of different periods and the circumstances in which the works of art were produced. The art of the Greeks from the 8th century BC seems, at first sight, to show an apparently simple, logical, and, indeed, inevitable development towards naturalism. It seems easy to divide into periods of preparation, high achievement and decline;

some think of an archaic statue (figure 7) as less developed and therefore inferior to a 5th-century figure (figure 24). The sculptures of the great temple of Zeus at Olympia (figure 15) have been called crude, the Laocoon group (figure 42) judged the greatest sculpture of all antiquity. Many such judgements, whether valid or not, are passed in ignorance of the whole development of classical art.

OUR KNOWLEDGE OF CLASSICAL ART

In fact, it is only since the 19th century that a reasonably complete picture of classical art has been possible. With the collapse of the ancient world, most of the great masterpieces of painting and sculpture were lost and they will never be recovered. Bronzes were melted down, paintings destroyed, marble sculpture burnt for lime; the great buildings survived only because they could be put to new practical uses. A thousand years later the Italian Renaissance found inspiration in antique art and began to study it. Artists and writers found everything in antiquity excellent and perfect, but the classical art they knew was a very little part of the whole, and without the Greek background they could hardly judge the merit, and certainly not the originality, of the Roman works they did see. In the 18th century the scientific study of classical art was inspired by the great Winckelmann, but he knew no original Greek masterpiece, no single work of the archaic period, and could not yet master the chronological sequence of the surviving pieces. Few today would share the unqualified praise he gave to the first statues recovered from the buried town of Herculaneum in 1711, or accept the judgement of his contemporary, the Marchese Venuti, on a painting of Theseus and the Minotaur from Pompeii as 'the loveliest thing in the world, much more beautiful than the work of Raphael'. The marbles, as we now know, were mechanical copies of Greek works, and the wall-paintings made by artisans inspired by masterpieces of the past. We cannot share with the 18th century this wholehearted admiration for the 'Greco-Roman' schools, because since the 19th century the excavation of Greek sites has given us a more thorough picture of the development of art and architecture in classical lands. And yet it must be remembered that this picture remains a very partial one. The position is still that we have only two or three works by sculptors who were famous in antiquity, and that we cannot enjoy a single famous painting. It is true that we know something of them from copies made in Roman times, but the copy is no real substitute for the original. There are still periods for which our knowledge of artistic development is slight, and for which the evidence is likely to remain poor. After Pompeii, for example, the surviving examples of Roman decorative painting are meagre. New discoveries, of course, continue to be made for all periods, and will improve the knowledge we have at present.

The Character of Greek Art

The place of art in the life of the Greeks, at least until the Hellenistic period, was very different from our own. Early Greek art always had a practical purpose, whether to adorn the temples of the gods or to decorate a pot. At all levels of activity, the artist was looked upon as a useful member of society who was respected for his skill as a craftsman. Art was a completely professional activity in the best sense of the word, and because it maintained a generally high level of craftsmanship, Greek art seems to throw up masterpieces, and certainly works of immense skill, at a comparatively humble level—a superbly drawn picture on a vase, an exquisite figure on a bronze mirror. The craftsman underwent a long training in the workshop of his master, and this, no doubt, does much to explain the strongly conservative character of Greek art as a whole, and the fact that a limited number of themes in sculpture, painting and architecture underwent comparatively little change over a long period.

But although, as we are often reminded, the Greeks had no word for *art* as opposed to *craft*, they recognised that great art is much more than a distinguished example of technical skill, and that it owes its greatness to the creative power of the artist. The sculptor Pheidias, in his statues of the Olympian gods, was held to have added something to the Olympian religion; Polykleitos to have incorporated art itself in his statues of men. In the 5th century BC it was believed that the purpose of art was to edify, to create perfect forms of men and gods, and to illustrate the noble themes that expressed the triumph of Greek civilisation over barbarism. The ancient world believed that Greek ideals, based on the concept of perfect form, had been completely achieved in the second half of the 5th century BC. The Parthenon (figure 20) was surely the greatest of Doric temples; the work of the 5th-century sculptors showed the perfect harmony of ideal form and nature in the representation of the human figure.

The 4th century, and the Hellenistic period that followed, changed the whole character of Greek art. While recognising the unapproachable perfection of the 5th-century ideal, it turned its attention to aspects of art that had been neglected. If it criticised earlier art, it was for its lack of variety, and it ranged for inspiration over the whole field of nature and humanity, and began to treat themes which had either been deliberately ignored or never approached in the earlier period. The rise of portraiture is the most obvious example of this new development, but the period also gave rise to all the *genres* of painting and sculpture which are now part of western artistic tradition, and to the full development of techniques. The conditions of the time, whereby the artist could travel widely and find employment with rich patrons over the vastly enlarged Greek world, gave new opportunities for the spread of ideas and techniques. The respect for the past also gave rise to our modern conception of a 'work of art', that is to say, of a work which is respected not for any practical reasons but solely for its beauty and fame. We find the Hellenistic kings building up art collections as such; the kings of Pergamon in the 2nd century BC had copies made of famous 'masterpieces', and paid enormous sums for Greek paintings. Two distinct traditions began to form; a living tradition, which carries on the story of classical art, tackling new problems and subjects and developing new techniques, and a 'classicising' tradition, which looks back to the art of the 5th and 4th centuries as a direct source of inspiration.

GREEK ART AND THE ROMANS

The Romans in the 2nd century BC inherited the artistic patronage of the Hellenistic kings. As their enthusiasm for Greek art developed, the two traditions became clearly and firmly established. On the one hand, as 'connoisseurs' of the antique they collected originals of the famous masterpieces and encouraged new and flourishing schools of copyists; in this direction they called for almost nothing new, except eclectic works which combined the most popular features of a number of favoured schools. On the other hand, they, like the Hellenistic kings, gave their patronage to Greek artists and craftsmen who were to carve statues, paint pictures and erect buildings in Rome and Italy. At first their patronage was given with a sense of guilt, which gets its positive expression in the attitude of such Romans of the old school as Marcus Porcius Cato the censor, who led the attack on luxury and the taste for things Greek. But under the Emperor Augustus came the full rapprochement between the traditionally Roman ideas and Greek art. Just as Virgil's *Aeneid* is a Roman epic for all that much of its inspiration is Greek, so the *Ara Pacis* is a Roman monument though its sculptors and much of its style was Greek.

The choice of the philhellene Romans ensured the survival of the Greek artistic tradition through the period of the Empire. Nor indeed should we underestimate the power of the Romans to develop and add to that tradition. We have to acknowledge that it is to the Romans that we owe not only a great part of our knowledge of Greek art, but the creation of a 'classical tradition' in art. The buildings and the sculptured monuments of the Empire are far different from those of the Greeks, but they make creative use of Greek motifs and, at least until the end of the 2nd century AD, the Romans maintained a wholehearted respect for Greek form in sculpture and painting. From the first we see important differences of taste between Greek and Roman, and as the Empire progresses, there appear new ideas, religious and artistic, which are directly opposed to the classical. The conflict between classical and anti-classical modes of representational art in the late Empire forms a fascinating study. The anti-classical triumphs in the Byzantine style, but the classical survives as a source of inspiration and triumphs again in the civilisation of the Renaissance in Italy.

Historical Outline

BRONZE AGE CRETE

The first flowering of civilisation in Greek lands took place in Minoan Crete, the Crete of the legendary King Minos, whose rediscovery is the achievement of our own century. The understanding of metals, reaching the Aegean from the Near East, made this civilisation possible, and it flourished from the 3rd millennium BC until about 1400 BC. About 2000 BC, the lords of the Minoan cities built large palaces in several places on the island, the best known being the great palace of Minos at Knossos. Their wealth and prosperity provided the resources for monumental building and creative artistic achievement, which finds its best expression in colourful decorative painting, lively and naturalistic sculpture on a small scale, exquisite work in gem-engraving and precious metalwork.

THE MYCENAEAN GREEKS

About the same time that the palaces were built in Crete, the first Greek-speaking people arrived on the mainland of Greece. By about 1600 they, too, had become powerful and wealthy; the first manifestation of what we call Mycenaean culture is seen in the lordly burials of the so-called Shaft Graves of Mycenae, excavated by Schliemann in the late 19th century. Mycenaean civilisation was far different from Cretan. Mycenaean sites are strongly fortified citadels ruled over by feudal lords. Their architecture had little in common with that of their Cretan neighbours, but for the arts of painting and sculpture the Mycenaeans turned to Crete. Cretan artists decorated the halls of their palaces, made vases and other objects of luxury. By 1400, it seems, the Mycenaeans had conquered Crete, usurped its power in the Aegean, and asserted their influence over the whole Mediterranean world. During the most flourishing period of Mycenaean power, from 1400–1200 BC, tendencies in their art and certain specific art-forms seem to have an unequivocal connection with Greek art in its later phases. There are definite connections between later Mycenaean architectural designs and the buildings of classical Greece, and perhaps some positive signs of the emergence of new artistic ideas in painting and sculpture. But all this was cut short by the collapse of the Mycenaean world in the 12th century, and there followed a period of poverty and obscurity that is known as the Greek Dark Ages.

THE DEVELOPMENT OF GREEK CIVILISATION

During the period of obscurity the historical Greek world took shape. The destruction of the Mycenaean towns and citadels is associated with an invasion from the north—the Dorian invasion—of further Greek-speaking people. This invasion, which destroyed Mycenaean culture, also produced large-scale migration of Greeks from the mainland across the Aegean Sea to found the later Greek cities on the coast of Asia Minor and establish the pattern of settlement there in historical times. Although all the luxury arts ceased in the Dark Ages, there was a continuous tradition of decorated pottery which is also our principal historical docu-

ment for the period. The 'proto-geometric' style of pottery-decoration seems to have originated in Athens around 1000 BC, and is characterised by abstract ornament, consisting of carefully organised geometric patterns, which forms the basis of the subsequent development of Greek art.

When the feudal system of the Mycenaean world came to an end, the geographical divisions of the Greek mainland asserted themselves, and gave rise to the kind of community we call the city-state and the Greeks themselves called *polis*, an urban centre controlling a surrounding countryside enclosed in the mountains and high hills that divide the country. Royal government gave way to aristocracy, and by the time the Greeks re-emerge into history all the essential conditions of Greek life are there. The links with the Mycenaean world are strong. The Greek epic, which was to be a main source of inspiration for Greek art, had descended through the centuries, and the Olympian religion had taken shape as the communal religion of the city-states.

By the 8th century BC the Greek city-states, ruled over by hereditary aristocracies, had recovered much of their prosperity, and began a period of expansion by trade and colonisation in the Mediterranean. With increased wealth and prosperity came the first attempts at monumental art; the enormous funerary vases of the developed geometric style in Athens, the movement towards temple-building, and very soon the making of large cult-images of the gods. In the late-geometric style the human figure again became part of the repertory of representational art, and there are narrative scenes which seem to be inspired by Homeric epic, themes which run right through the history of classical art. From this time onwards the development of classical art is clear and continuous.

THE GREEK EXPANSION

This development is strongly conditioned by historical circumstances. In the 7th century Greek trade and colonisation brought the city-states into close contact with the civilisations of the ancient east. In Egypt, Greeks saw the gigantic temples and cult-images of the Pharaohs, and their earliest large-scale statues made about the middle of the century were chiefly inspired by what they saw. So thoroughgoing is the influence of oriental art in this period, that the phase of Greek art which follows the geometric of the 9th and 8th centuries is normally called the 'orientalising'. But oriental themes were not merely adopted into Greek art; they were adapted into a living and developing tradition.

Commercial prosperity created problems for the governing aristocracies of the Greek cities. It produced a class of rich merchants important to the well-being of the state, but lacking a major voice in its government; the peasant-farmer, too, was often discontented. Conditions were thus created for revolutionary activity which, in fact, happened in most of the city-states during the 6th century. Throughout the early archaic period the wealthy aristocrats were the chief patrons of the arts; in the revolutionary period their place was often taken by the 'tyrant', a man, generally from the ranks of the rich merchants, who rose to power by championing the discontented elements in the city-states. The Athens of Pisistratus, one of the most famous of these tyrants, was rich and colourful; a tremendous stimulus to artistic achievement was given by the court of this tyrant, producing conditions which we do not meet again until the court patronage of the Hellenistic kings.

THE CITY–STATES

Tyranny was succeeded in many city-states by a form of democracy, such as that which ruled Athens during her period of greatness in the 5th century. The Athenian democracy was established at the end of the 6th century, and it was under this form of government that she made her contribution to the combined effort of the city-states against the invasions of the Persians. The result enormously increased her prestige and gave her the leadership of the alliance designed to protect the Greek cities, especially those of the Asiatic coast and the islands, against Persian power. The Persian wars also provided the complete break with the traditions of archaic art. There is no greater contrast than that between the decorative prettiness of the figures of maidens dedicated on the Acropolis in the last years of the 6th century, and the severity of the sculptured female figure of the years that followed the war. The self-confident ideals of the city-states, now the chief patrons of the arts, find their greatest expression in Pericles' ambitious building projects on the Acropolis at Athens.

The Peloponnesian War destroyed the city-states, breaking their political vigour, undermining the faith in the old gods, encouraging individualism and private luxury. Whereas the art of the 5th century seems an expression of the whole society in which it was created, and the artist a willing servant of its religious and social life, the aims and ideals of the 4th century are less clearly defined. The limited perfection of ideal form achieved in the 5th century fails to satisfy, the Olympian religion ceases to inspire. The gods of Praxiteles shed their majesty and become elegant and human creatures. Increasing individualism is reflected in the rise of portraiture. The economic decline of the city-states persuaded more Greek artists to find work abroad among the wealthy barbarians on the fringes of their world. The artist no longer worked for the small communities of Greece, but travelled widely. His independent status was increasingly recognised by the patrons of the day. Although major works of art were still largely financed by the state, few large building schemes were carried out in Greece itself.

THE HELLENISTIC WORLD

From the middle of the 4th century, the kingdom of Macedon under Philip and his son Alexander became the centre of Greek culture. Macedon emerged as the champion of the city-states, against the will of most of them, and Alexander's conquests in the east opened up a new world to Greek civilisation. Alexander's dreams of a cosmopolitan Greek culture were never achieved, but the world of his successors was vastly more cosmopolitan than that of the classical Greeks. The new kingdoms of the Seleucids in Syria and the Ptolemies in Egypt were founded in eastern countries and the semi-Hellenised rulers held sway as far afield as India. Hellenistic art takes much of its character from this new situation. Art is again placed at the service of private patronage, and in the process becomes largely divorced from religious and political life. Great political events can still inspire grandiose artistic schemes, but, in the main, the artists' themes are secular and often personal, they go their own way, developing new techniques and searching for themes among all races and ages and from the whole range of human emotions.

THE RISE OF ROME

By the 2nd century BC Rome had asserted her rule over most of the Italian peninsula. The defeat of Carthage in the Second Punic War brought her into increasingly close contact with the Hellenistic kingdoms and, one by one, they succumbed to her power. By the time of Augustus the Romans had built up an empire stretching from Spain to Syria, controlled by a uniform system of government which survived for 300 years. In the history of art, Rome's enthusiastic adoption of Greek art is an event of the utmost importance. The Greek colonies in South Italy and Sicily and the philhellene tastes of the Etruscans had already laid the basis for the spread of Greek culture; and the Roman Empire, backed by a strong system of government, further extended it over large parts of Europe previously untouched by its influence. It brought the civilised world very close to the dream of cosmopolitan Greek culture conceived by Alexander the Great. The Romans ensured the survival of the Greek tradition, and it is the measure of the strength of that tradition that Christianity, originating among the Jews of Roman Palestine, developing under the influence of oriental mysticism, and violently protesting against pagan ideals, yet continued to draw inspiration from pagan art.

The Bronze Age

THE BRONZE AGE AND HISTORICAL GREECE

Books on Greek art do not always include the Bronze Age, and some still deliberately and firmly refuse to take it into account. The art of Minoan Crete seems at first sight so alien to that of the historical Greeks that the recently expressed view that 'European pictorial art begins with the Minoans' seems completely indefensible. For the moment we may leave this question aside. Nowadays, the study of the Bronze Age as a prelude to classical art seems, in any case, inevitable. Since Schliemann excavated at Mycenae at the end of the 19th century, the historical basis of the heroic age of Greece has been accepted as fact, and that heroic age provided the subject-matter for a great part of Greek art and literature. Since Ventris, much more recently, deciphered the script known as Linear B found in Crete and Mycenaean Greece, and established that the language is an early form of Greek, the student of classical Greece has to take his studies back at least to that time when it is believed that the Greek speakers first entered Greece, say about 1900 BC. And since archaeological discoveries in the Aegean area have shown the close connections between the art and civilisation of ancient Crete and that of the Mycenaean Greeks, we are almost forced to take up the story at that point when the civilisation of ancient Crete began to flourish.

THE ORIGINS OF CRETAN ART

Before the introduction of metals into Crete, the island was inhabited by people at the neolithic level of civilisation, living in agricultural communities. Art of a simple kind already had its place; pottery in everyday use was decorated with incised patterns, clay figures of humans and animals were being modelled by primitive artists. The introduction of metals about the middle of the 3rd millennium BC, began to transform the agricultural communities. Crete lies in a favoured position for trade with the eastern Mediterranean, from which the knowledge of working metals came. Egyptian influence is apparent in Crete from an early period and there are contacts, too, with the islands of the Cyclades and with Anatolia. Ivory scarabs and figures closely modelled on Egyptian prototypes have been found on the island, and some of the pottery forms seem to derive from Anatolia. Cycladic imports include the marble idols characteristic of the early Bronze Age in the Aegean. These idols (figure 1) reduce the human figure to a simple formula which makes a striking contrast with the spontaneous attempts at naturalism in neolithic figures, and it is surely significant that they are confined to the Aegean area, where many years later Greek art was to find its basis in a similar approach to the problems of representing the human figure.

Despite the strong foreign influences, Cretan art in this early period begins to show its own individual character. Decorative motifs, such as running spirals and meanders, increase the repertory of neolithic ornament on the early painted pottery, and one begins to appreciate the keen decorative sense of Cretan artists and their imaginative synthesis of form and decoration. The early figurines of clay and other materials are simple in form and structure, but already show a strong interest in movement and gesture. The favourite subjects for small-scale terracottas are animals and worshippers, male and female; the humans are already dressed like the Cretans we know from the later paintings and sculptures.

THE PALACES OF CRETE

By about 2000 BC the pattern of developed Cretan civilisation had taken shape. At this time the country seems to have been controlled by a number of powerful rulers, who built themselves the palaces which have become known to us as the result of excavations in this century. The Palace of Knossos was first built in this period, those of Mallia and Phaistos are not much later. Sir Arthur Evans, who first excavated and recreated Knossos, called the Bronze Age civilisation of Crete Minoan, after the legendary King Minos who ruled there. The Minoan palaces went through a long history of building and reconstruction from 2000 BC onwards, and their earliest form is not well known to us. But it seems that from the first they were planned on a fairly grand scale, and that the big central courtyard around which the buildings were grouped, at first perhaps in isolated blocks, is an original feature. They were well built of solid masonry, and probably made use of columnar architecture to support the roofs.

There is no major art of painting and sculpture associated with the palaces in their earliest form. The Minoan pottery of this period, however, is some of the most attractive that has survived from the ancient world, and the most imaginative in design. A variety of colours—orange, red, yellow and white—are used on the dark body of the vessel; the motifs are either patterns of purely abstract character or are based upon plant life. These versions of plant life, although they do not imitate nature, imply a keen understanding of its forms and they are applied quite brilliantly to the shapes they decorate. The big jar illustrated in plate 2 is exceptional in that a representation of a fish is used as a principal decorative motif; the strange bubble-like motif that seems to issue from the mouth of the fish has been variously interpreted in terms of nature, but it illustrates best of all the rich imagination of the Minoan decorative sense in this period. As time goes on there is a tendency to imitate nature more closely, and some of the seal-engravings, which are among the finest survivals of Minoan art, begin to show the lively naturalistic style that is associated with the great period of Minoan art.

THE LATER PALACES

Major rebuilding of most of the Cretan palaces around 1650 BC, after a catastrophe on the island, gave them the form in which we see them today. At Knossos, Sir Arthur Evans made a brave attempt to recreate the appearance of certain parts of the palace, replacing lost wooden columns with concrete ones, rebuilding rooms, staircases and light

1. **Cycladic idol.** 3rd millennium BC.
Marble. h. 19¼ in. (49 cm.). British
Museum, London. One of a large number of standing nude female figures made
in the islands of the Cyclades.

wells. Fragments of paintings found in the excavations were used to reconstruct the schemes of decoration on the walls; the total effect now is of a ruin which seems to be both ancient and modern at the same time. If you visit Knossos today it is an unforgettable but perplexing experience. You wander along corridors and from room to room without seeming to recall a stopping point; everywhere you see signs of comfortable, even luxurious, living, and relics of a courtly and religious life that is still hardly understood. The grand rooms of the state apartments on the west side of the courtyard have largely disappeared, except for some of the ground plan reconstructed by Evans; it is only on the east side, in what is believed to be the private apartments of the palace, that the pillared halls, the columned staircases, the light wells have been completely reconstructed. It is all a very far cry from the Greek world; only occasionally does the student of classical architecture feel at home with the reconstructed wooden columns, with their crowning members that seem to have something in common with the classical Doric. The wall paintings that decorated the rooms of the palace are our closest contact with the people who lived there. The view of the so-called Throne Room (plate 8) shows one of the attempts to reconstruct a complete decorative scheme from surviving fragments; similar attempts were made by Evans in other parts of the palace. These paintings give us some insight into the courtly life, the games and rituals of the people but they have come down to us in a tantalisingly fragmentary state.

CRETAN WALL-PAINTING

The techniques of wall-painting became known in Crete from Egypt and the eastern Mediterranean, but the Cretan paintings, most of which date from the period between 1600 and 1400 BC, are very different from Egyptian work. The techniques in use include painted stucco relief and true fresco-painting, that is, the application of colour to the plaster surface of the wall while it is still damp. The colours used have a limited range; strong reds, blues, greens and yellows are favoured. In scale the pictures range from the monumental to the miniature.

Among the earliest paintings, dating from about 1600 BC, is the one illustrated in plate 4, part of a room decorated with garden scenes in a villa at Amnisos on the coast, not far from Knossos. Three white lily flowers growing from a calyx of leaves are combined into an attractively simple design, that shows the same keen sense of decorative stylisation based upon natural forms that we have seen in earlier Cretan pottery. The most remarkable achievements of Cretan painters at this time are their attempts at vivid illustration of the world of men and nature. Their technique is limited, their range of colour small, their art lacks understanding of the principles of illusionistic painting. Their conventions are simple: man is red, woman is white. Figures, drawn with hard outlines and coloured with flat washes, are shown in profile, or awkwardly combining

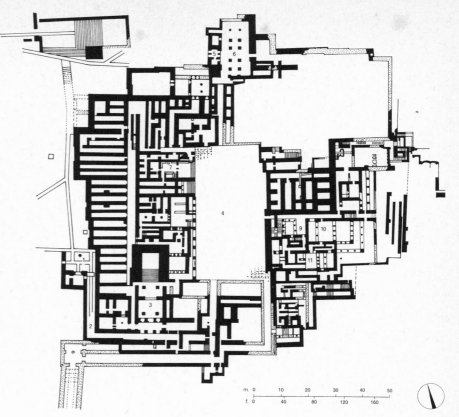

A. Plan of the Palace at Knossos.

1 West Porch

2 Corridor of the Procession

3 South Propylon

4 Central Court

5 North Propylon

6 Pillar Hall

7 Throne Room

8 Grand Staircase

9 Hall of the Colonnade

10 Hall of the Double Axes

11 Rooms of the Queen's Megaron

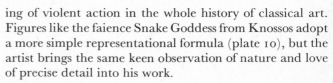

profile head and frontal body with profile legs. Yet, when they want to show action, the artists can do it with a spontaneous liveliness that is wholly convincing. Their studies of nature are keenly observed. It is an art which seems to be trying to run before it can walk, yet nothing seems to be beyond it. The fragments of a bull's head, over life size, from a painted relief that once decorated a loggia by the north entrance to the palace at Knossos is a brilliant study of the charging animal (plate 3). In the scene in plate 5, which comes from a painting in the miniature style, groups of spectators in an olive orchard are watching a festival of dancing, and here the artist adopts a racy, almost impressionistic use of colour to suggest the massed spectators. The achievement of Minoan painters during this period can be best appreciated if we compare their work with the representational art of the Greeks in the 6th century BC.

CRETAN SCULPTURE

The sculpture contemporary with these wall-paintings shows the same fine command of naturalistic detail and movement. The bull's head vase, or *rhyton*, of black steatite from Knossos is carved with absolutely confident three-dimensional plasticity (plate 9); an ivory figure of an acrobat from Knossos gives a wonderful portrayal of vigorous movement. On the well-known Harvester Vase from Hagia Triada, we find a clever study of the faces of the singing harvesters and a keen understanding of movement. Some of the most remarkable Cretan relief-work is to be seen on the two gold cups decorated with repoussé, which were found in a Tholos Tomb at Vaphio, in the Peloponnese, but are certainly Cretan work of the 15th century BC. A detail of one of these cups (figure 2) shows a striking scene where a bull has charged a hunter and a huntress, hurling one of them into the air. We shall not find a more effective rendering of violent action in the whole history of classical art. Figures like the faience Snake Goddess from Knossos adopt a more simple representational formula (plate 10), but the artist brings the same keen observation of nature and love of precise detail into his work.

LATER CRETAN PAINTING

The 'naturalistic' phase of Cretan art was short-lived, perhaps inevitably so. The potters of this period tried to apply the varied forms of nature to the decoration of the vessels, and were most brilliantly effective in the so-called 'marine style' illustrated by the Octopus Vase in plate 7. By about 1450 there are strong signs of new artistic influences in the pottery of Knossos. Vessels of the 'Palace Style' (plate 12) show a renewed attempt to reduce the world of nature to order and decorative symmetry, and, although the technique is different, the effect brings us back to something much closer to the early styles of Cretan pottery. The influence of Egyptian representational art shows more strongly in the later fresco-paintings, especially the processional scenes. There is a stiff formalism in the ritual scenes painted on the famous alabaster sarcophagus from Hagia Triada, which belongs to the 14th century BC (plate 14). The artists were clearly giving up their attempts at free imitation of nature; the age of Cretan naturalism was over.

The appearance of new artistic tendencies in Knossos around 1450 BC has been associated by some archaeologists with the arrival of Greeks from the mainland. Archaeological discoveries lend their support to this view, and in the graves of the period there is evidence for the presence of a more warlike people, such as we know the Mycenaean Greeks to have been. On one of the well-known vases of the 'Palace Style' there appears one of those boar's tusk helmets that are characteristic of the armour of the Myce-

2. **Cup from Vaphio.** *c.* 1500 BC. Gold. h. 3½ in. (9 cm.). National Museum, Athens. One of a pair of gold cups, with repoussé reliefs, found in a Tholos tomb at Vaphio, in Laconia. The scene illustrated here shows a bull attacking a hunter and huntress.

naeans. Not long after, the supposed appearance of the Mycenaeans the palace of Knossos was destroyed—according to the still prevailing view, around 1400 BC. At this point we must turn from Crete to the mainland of Greece and consider the earlier development of the people of the mainland who, it seems, had usurped the power of the Minoans in the Aegean world.

THE EARLY BRONZE AGE IN GREECE

The Early Bronze Age on the mainland of Greece is known as Early Helladic, and it began rather later than the Bronze Age in Crete. Its character, too, is quite different, the closest affinities being with the Greek islands and the Bronze Age in Anatolia. The characteristic pottery shapes associated with the phase, the 'sauceboat' and the two-handled goblet, are also found at Troy and other Anatolian sites, and probably originated there. There are close connections, too, between the architecture of the two areas. The *megaron* house, which was to be the most important single unit of the later Mycenaean palace, is found in both areas. The Middle Helladic phase, which begins early in the second millennium, is associated with an invasion of new peoples who are now generally believed to be the first Greek speakers to arrive in the Greek peninsula. The Middle Helladic invaders introduced new architectural forms, though some of the old were still retained, new burial customs and new types of pottery. They built on the same sites as those which were later to be important as Mycenaean citadels. The general level of prosperity seems to have been lower than that of the Early Helladic phase but, by 1600, a general accession of wealth created the early Mycenaean culture which is known to us chiefly from the remarkable finds made by Schliemann in the Shaft Graves of the famous Grave Circle at Mycenae, and

from those in the more recently discovered second Grave Circle at the same place.

THE SHAFT GRAVES OF MYCENAE

The Shaft Graves are a series of rectangular burials cut in the rock, with walls of rubble masonry and roofs of timber and stone slabs. When, later, the massive 14th-century walls of Mycenae were built, the burials were enclosed by circles of close-set upright stone slabs (figure 3). The burials, especially those in Schliemann's Circle, were accompanied by rich possessions, which suggest that they must have been the burials of the Royal House of Mycenae. We know very little of the citadel in which these Mycenaeans lived, since the walls and palace of Mycenae belong to a later phase, but they themselves come before us with a remarkable immediacy in the series of forbiddingly regal death masks of gold plate, which were laid upon the faces of the men; even if, as we now know, these men lived long before the Achaean lords of Homer's epic, we feel much more at home with them than with the Minoans. Their warlike character, their love of hunting, so clearly reflected in the contents of the tombs, put us in mind of Homer's heroes.

The objects found in the Shaft Graves are the personal possessions of the dead. The men are buried with their richly decorated weapons and vessels of precious metal; the women wore extravagant jewellery and had vessels of gold and silver for their own use. Because the decoration of these objects is predominantly Minoan in character, it was once thought that they represented loot taken by the Mycenaean lords from Crete, but a closer analysis of the finds has shown that while many of the objects are obviously the work of Minoan craftsmen, they are made to Mycenaean usage and taste. Shaft Grave art can be considered Minoan in the same sense that Roman art is Greek; the Mycenaeans em-

3. The grave circle at Mycenae.
14th century BC. diam. 90 ft. (27.5 m.).
The double ring of upright slabs was put
up to enclose the Shaft Graves of a dynasty
of Mycenaean kings, buried between 1600
and 1500 BC.

ployed Cretan artists, but they asked them to illustrate themes and decorate objects that suited a different taste. We must suppose that an artist from Crete came to the mainland to decorate the superb inlaid dagger illustrated in plate 16. The scene, which is inlaid with gold, silver and niello on a copper sheet fixed to the dagger, shows an episode in a lion hunt in which four soldiers and an archer are in combat with the lion, who has already struck down one of them. It is a wonderfully vigorous, if exaggerated, scene of action that must be the work of a fine Cretan craftsman. Prosperity gave the Mycenaean lords the opportunity to employ the best Cretan skill in all branches of the arts, and so to satisfy their admiration for the arts and crafts of a superior civilisation.

THE CITADELS OF THE MYCENAEAN WORLD

The great period of the Mycenaean world begins about 1400, at just the time when it is believed that the palace of Knossos was finally destroyed. By this time the Mycenaeans had become the principal power in the Aegean, they had trading contacts not only with the eastern and western Mediterranean, but also with central Europe, and they colonised widely in their sphere of influence. The great citadels at Mycenae (plate 17), Tiryns and elsewhere, took the shape in which we know them today during the 14th century. The sites are characterised by massive defensive walls built to enclose the palace of the king, and to be a place of refuge in time of trouble. These walls are built either of large squared blocks of regular masonry, or of rough hewn blocks of enormous size carefully fitted together so as to give the appearance of a level surface; the classical Greeks believed that the giant Cyclops built the walls, and justifiably. At Tiryns, 'the most Cyclopean walls in all Greece' were as much as 17½ metres thick at one point in their circuit (plate 20). The great Lion Gate at Mycenae (figure 4), which forms the main entrance to the citadel provides us with the first example from the Greek world of monumental sculpture allied to architecture. As we have seen, there was no monumental sculpture in the Minoan world, but here the massive entrance, with its enormous stone lintel, is surmounted by a relief that shows two lions heraldically flanking a column and entablature, which symbolise the palace of Mycenae. The lions and the column are Minoan in character, but the scale of the architectural conception is Mycenaean.

(Continued on page 33)

1. **Early-Cycladic head.** 3rd millennium
BC. Marble. h. 11½ in. (29 cm.). National
Museum, Athens. This head, from a large
marble idol of the type illustrated in fig. 1,
was found on the island of Amorgos in the
Cyclades. Idols of this type were made
in many of the Cycladic islands during
this period.

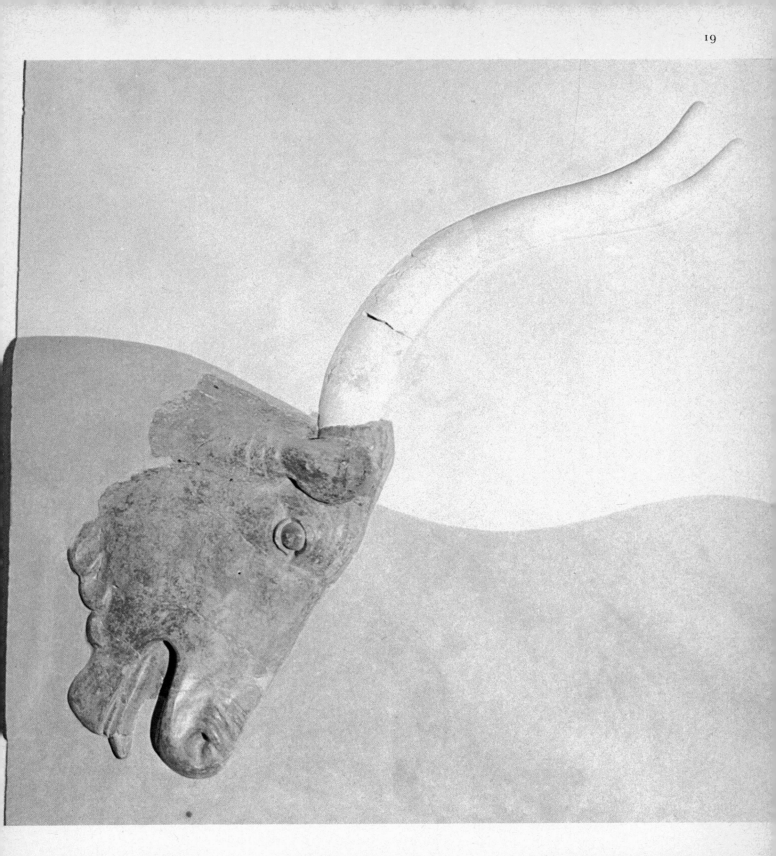

2. (left). **Jar from Phaistos.** 1900–1700 BC. Pottery. h. 20 in. (50 cm.). Heraklion Museum, Crete. The design, based on curvilinear patterns, incorporates a representation of a fish shown with what looks like an enormous bubble issuing from its mouth; the hatching may be intended for the mesh of a net. In this early Cretan style of pottery decoration, representations of the animal world are rare, though many of the decorative motifs are based upon natural forms. The spiral patterns are typical of Cretan decorative art.

3. (above). **Bull's head relief painting from Knossos.** Early 16th century BC. Painted plaster. h. 17½ in. (44 cm.). Heraklion Museum, Crete. This fragment, a magnificent example of Cretan naturalism, is part of a large composition which decorated the loggia at the north entrance to the Palace of Knossos. Painted relief is one of the earlier techniques used by Cretan wall-painters.

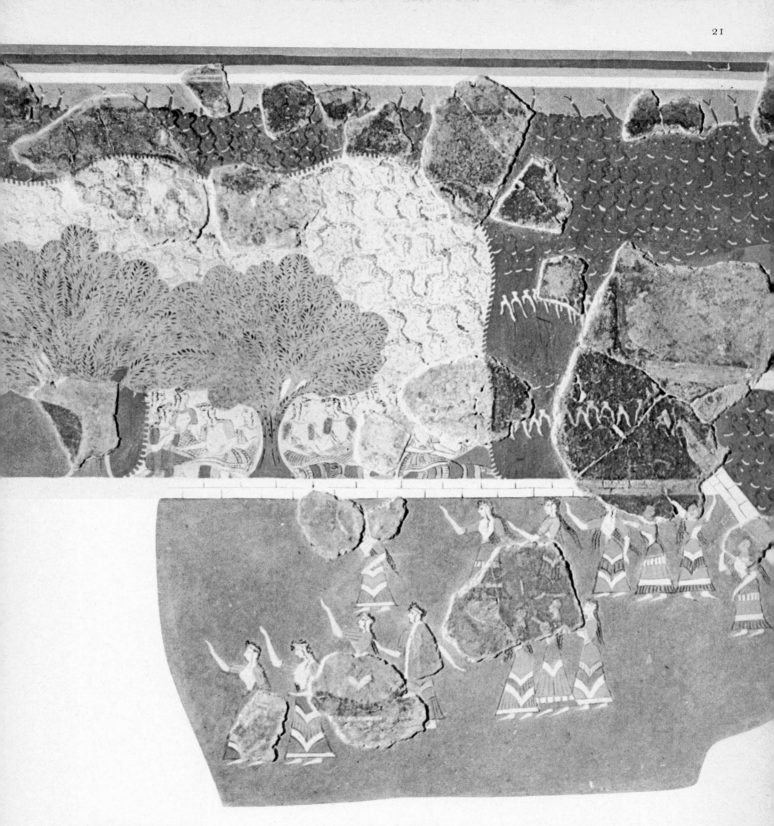

4. (left). **White lilies in a garden.**
c. 1600 BC. Fresco. h. 6 ft. 3 in. (1.89 m.).
Heraklion Museum, Crete. Wall painting
from a Villa at Amnisos near Knossos.
The design consists of three white lilies
growing from a calyx of leaves. This
painting is one of the earliest examples
of Minoan fresco painting.

5. (above). **Miniature fresco of olive
trees and dancers from Knossos.**
c. 1450 BC. Fresco. approx. h. 14 in.
(35 cm.). Heraklion Museum, Crete.
The scene shows groups of spectators
sitting among olive trees and watching
women perform a ritual dance. The
'impressionistic' method of suggesting a
crowd is interesting: for the men, patches

of reddish-brown colour with a series of
heads roughly painted; for the women,
patches of white with similar sketchy
drawing of the heads.

6. (above). **Painting of flying fish from Melos.** 15th century BC. Fresco. h. 9 in. (23 cm.). National Museum, Athens. This fresco was found in the palace of Phylakopi on the island of Melos. The painting, which is certainly the work of a Cretan artist, is a fine example of the combination of keen observation of nature and strong decorative sense that characterises all the best Cretan painting.

7. (left). **Octopus vase.** *c.* 1500 BC. Pottery. h. 11¼ in. (28 cm.). Heraklion Museum, Crete. This little flask, of a type normally called a 'stirrup jar', was found at Palaikastro in eastern Crete. It is a fine example of the 'marine-style' of Cretan pot-painting. The surface of the vase is painted with a representation of an octopus swimming amid seaweed, coral and shells: a lively naturalism is combined with a superb decorative sense.

8. (right). **The Throne Room at Knossos.** This lies on the west side of the central court. The room is furnished with stone benches round the walls and a high-backed throne of alabaster. The paintings showing griffins in a landscape are modern reconstructions based upon fragments found in the excavations. The decoration of the throne room belongs to a late period of the Palace.

9. (below). **Bull's head rhyton from Knossos.** *c.* 1500 BC. Black steatite. h. 10½ in. (26 cm.). Heraklion Museum, Crete. Ritual vessel carved in the form of a bull's head. The horns are gilded and the eyes are of rock crystal. The head, which is somewhat restored, is one of the most convincing pieces of Cretan naturalistic sculpture. It was found in the Little Palace at Knossos.

10. (right). **Snake Goddess.** *c.* 1600 BC. Faience. h. 17½ in. (29.5 cm.). Heraklion Museum, Crete. This statuette of a female figure holding snakes in both hands was found in the palace at Knossos. It is disputed whether she represents a goddess, queen or priestess. She wears the characteristic costume of Cretan women of the court, with breasts exposed, a tight waist, and long flounced skirt.

11. (below). **Palace of Knossos.** View of part of the royal apartments in the eastern wing of the Palace of Minos at Knossos. In this area it proved possible to restore rooms to something like their original appearance. The red columns, with their black cushion capitals, which support the staircase are reconstructions in concrete of original wooden columns. The rooms of this area seem to be private apartments; reception rooms, bedrooms, bath rooms and water-closets have been identified.

12. (left). **Palace style jar from Knossos.** *c.* 1450 BC. Pottery. approx. h. 3 ft. 3 in. (1.0 m.). Heraklion Museum, Crete. This large storage jar is decorated with a design of double-axes and plant ornament. The jar is very largely restoration, but illustrates well the so-called 'Palace style' that prevailed at Knossos around 1450 BC, in which decorative naturalism gives place to more formal designs.

13. (right). **Late Minoan figures of goddesses or votaries from Gazi.** 13th century BC. Terracotta. Larger figure: h. 2 ft. 6¼ in. (77 cm.). Heraklion Museum, Crete. These idols belong to the period after the collapse of Minoan power. A simple schematic form with cylindrical lower body has superseded the naturalism of earlier Cretan sculpture.

14. (below). **Sarcophagus from Hagia Triada.** *c.* 1400 BC. Alabaster. l. 4 ft. 6 in. (1.37 m.). National Museum, Athens. A small sarcophagus of alabaster with painted scenes on all four sides found at Hagia Triada, the royal villa not far from Phaistos. On the side illustrated here, the scene on the left shows two women

bringing libations to a shrine marked by two double axes. They are accompanied by a man playing a lyre. On the right three men are bringing offerings to an image standing in front of a building.

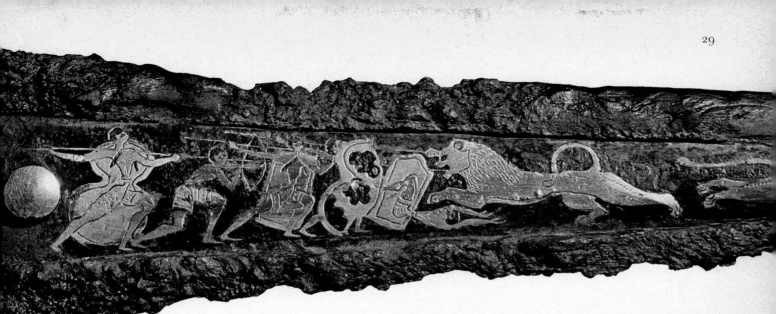

15. (left). **Head of a woman from Tiryns.** 13th century BC. Fresco. h. 12 in. (30.5 cm.). National Museum, Athens. This fine fragment of painting comes from a processional frieze which decorated the interior of the palace at Tiryns. The woman's dress and the style of the painting are Cretan, but the face is Mycenaean Greek with a marked similarity to the faces of Greek women of the archaic period.

16. (above). **Bronze dagger blade.** 16th century BC. Gold, silver and niello inlay on copper decorating the bronze. l. 9¼ in. (23.8 cm.). National Museum, Athens. The design inlaid on the dagger blade shows four soldiers and an archer fighting with a lion. One of the soldiers has been struck down by the lion which is already wounded by a spear. The style is Minoan and the dagger is probably the work of a Minoan craftsman. Found in the Fourth Shaft Grave at Mycenae.

17. (below). **A view of the citadel of Mycenae.** The site of Mycenae lies on the north side of the plain of Argos; the peak of Mount Prophetas Elias towers above it. This most famous of Mycenaean citadels stood in a well-defended strategic position and was protected by powerful fortification walls built in the 14th century BC. The palace buildings are on the summit of the hill.

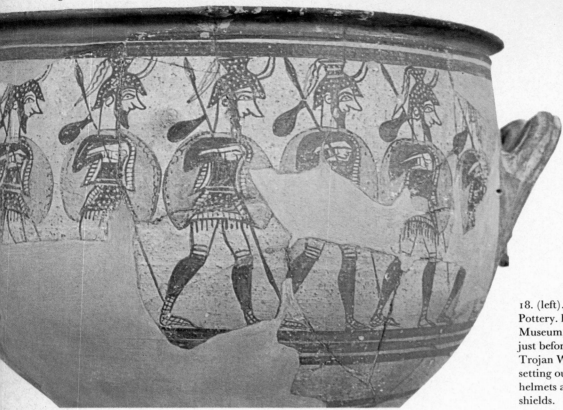

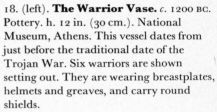

18. (left). **The Warrior Vase.** *c.* 1200 BC. Pottery. h. 12 in. (30 cm.). National Museum, Athens. This vessel dates from just before the traditional date of the Trojan War. Six warriors are shown setting out. They are wearing breastplates, helmets and greaves, and carry round shields.

19. (bottom left). **Foundations of Palace buildings at Tiryns.** 13th century BC. The plan of the Palace buildings at Tiryns is better preserved than at Mycenae. Of the megaron, the central hearth and base of the throne still survive and considerable remains of the rich interior decoration, including a painted floor and wall-frescoes, have come to light in excavations. The megaron was approached through a series of entrances and court-yards. The courtyard immediately in front of the megaron had a covered portico along three sides and in the open area stood an altar.

20. (below). **The walls of Tiryns.** 13th century BC. The Mycenaean citadel of Tiryns was built on a long narrow ridge rising from the plain of Argos, not far from Mycenae. The walls enclose the palace of the ruler and an area that served as a place of refuge in time of trouble; they were built during the most flourishing period of Mycenaean civilisation and were described by Pausanias as 'the most Cyclopean walls in Greece'. Some of the blocks used in the masonry are as much as 9 ft. long.

21. **Late Helladic crater from Cyprus.**
c. 1350 BC. Pottery. h. 16½ in. (42 cm.).
British Museum, London. This vessel of
the later Mycenaean period was found at
Maroni in Cyprus. The main frieze depicts
a pair of two-horse chariots, each with
two riders. Vases of this class, known as
Levanto-Helladic, illustrate well the
debased figure style of the late Mycenaean
period.

PALACES AND TOMBS

These grand architectural schemes are the chief Mycenaean contribution to the history of art. At first sight, the remains of the palaces themselves are disappointing. Tiryns is the best preserved, and here only the ground plan can be seen by the visitor (plate 19). The main characteristic feature is the *megaron*, a house form which had a long history on the Greek mainland and in Anatolia. A megaron generally consists of three elements—an open porch with columns supporting the entrance, an ante-chamber, and a main rectangular hall with a central hearth, which was both the reception and living room of the king; the roof of the megaron was supported by four columns. At Tiryns the megaron was approached through a series of courtyards and columned entrances, or *propylaea;* the main courtyard was surrounded by colonnades. The whole plan is much more closely related to classical Greek practice than anything we have seen at Knossos, and other sites in Crete.

The palace buildings were richly decorated with frescoes in Minoan technique, but often with a subject-matter that is Mycenaean. The megaron of Mycenae had frescoes showing battle subjects; at Pylos, scenes of peace and war were apparently combined. In the palace of Tiryns the paintings included purely decorative themes, among them a frieze of enormous figure-of-eight shields, and a processional frieze of women clad, apparently, in Minoan court dress. The head of one woman is illustrated in plate 15. The studied simplicity and clarity of outline seems to take us away from the spontaneous naturalism of Cretan painting and much closer to archaic Greek art; and it is remarkable how like an archaic Greek woman this Mycenaean looks.

The great chamber tombs at Mycenae and elsewhere are the most striking achievements of Mycenaean architecture. The use of corbelled vaulting, which we see in the galleries of the citadel of Tiryns, was applied with masterly effect to create a domed chamber on a circular plan. The so-called Treasury of Atreus, the most famous of these tombs at Mycenae, is 14.5 metres in diameter and the pointed dome (figure 5) rises to a height of 13.2 metres. The corbels are cut so as to give the effect of a continuous vault. The entrance to the tomb, which clearly served as a communal burial place for the rulers of Mycenae in the 14th century, is approached by a long passage cut in the rock; the entrance itself was decorated with applied architecture of coloured stones consisting of richly ornamented columns, on either side of the door, supporting an elaborate entablature. Fragments of the architecture can now be seen in the British Museum.

CRETAN AND MYCENAEAN ART

Throughout the period of Mycenaean power, the influence of Cretan art and technique dominates the courtly art, not only of painting but of precious metalwork and jewellery. It is in the more humble products of the potter's craft that fundamental changes of artistic outlook can best be seen, and they are changes which many people think show us the

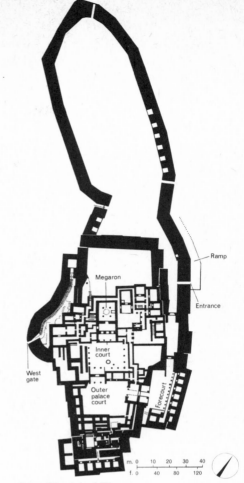

B. Plan of the Citadel of Tiryns.

4. **The Lion Gate, Mycenae.** 14th century BC. The main entrance to the citadel of Mycenae, with the famous relief over the lintel showing two lions flanking a column.

emergent Greek artistic spirit. The abandonment of natural forms in favour of a more stylised kind of ornament has already been seen in the pottery of the so-called Palace Style at Knossos, and in later Mycenaean times this tendency develops until we find decorative motifs whose naturalistic basis is scarcely recognisable, and those which are frankly based on abstract geometric patterns. Some of the latter look remarkably like the geometric decoration that characterises the pottery decoration of post-Mycenaean times, until one realises that they lack the rigid symmetry and precise execution of the later style.

Another striking anticipation of later Greek art is the appearance on late Mycenaean vases, of figure scenes arranged in a frieze zone round the body of the vessel. The well-known warrior vase from Mycenae (plate 18) shows a column of soldiers setting out; on the extreme left is the figure of a woman who bids them farewell. This vase, which was made about 1200 BC, seems to bring us very near to our image of the Achaeans who fought the Trojan War. The vases of the so-called Levanto-Helladic class, made in the 13th century BC, illustrate similar themes; an example from Cyprus in the British Museum (plate 21) shows the kind of decadent naturalism that seems to be leading inevitably to that complete extinction of representational art which, in fact, took place in the final collapse of the Mycenaean world. The conflicting tendencies in later Mycenaean art make it very hard to understand. On the one hand, we see the precarious survival of a naturalistic art based on the achievements of Cretan artists, and on the other, the emergence of a new taste for the order and simplicity of abstract forms.

THE END OF THE MYCENAEAN WORLD

The Mycenaean world came to an end about 1100 BC. The great palaces were destroyed, overseas connections were broken, and the whole system of Mycenaean rule collapsed. We have to consider in the next chapter what happened afterwards, but here we must consider the significance of the Bronze Age world in terms of the history of Greek art, and justify the inclusion of this chapter in a book on classical art. The Cretans, we know, were not Greeks, and this surely is clear in their art. The Greeks began their search for ideal form in art on the basis of a severely ordered sense of form to which the study of nature was secondary. The Minoans, on the other hand, drew their first inspiration from nature and, although they did not always imitate it, they were always acutely aware of it. The contrast between the Minoan and the Greek spirit goes deep. Nothing could be further from the ordered symmetry of Greek architecture than the informal, apparently haphazard, planning of the Minoan palaces. Indeed, we should not find it necessary to preface an account of 'classical art' with a Minoan chapter, if the Mycenaean world had not inherited the art of the Cretans, and applied it to their own purposes.

The Mycenaeans, as we know, were Greeks and, for all that, much of their art is Minoan in inspiration, they are very close to the Greeks of history. They created a monumental architecture that has much in common with Greek architecture. No one can look at the ground plan of the palace of Tiryns, with its ordered succession of courtyards and entrances leading to the megaron, without thinking of classical planning. The megaron form, itself, is connected with that of the later Greek temple; perhaps this is because many of the Acropolis sites were quickly converted into sanctuaries of the gods, as happened in the case of the palace at Tiryns. Much of the Mycenaean world did not survive, and only a memory of it, often false in detail, is preserved in the poems of Homer; Mycenaean writing disappeared completely. But if the art whose origins we are going to discuss in the next chapter is the product of a new creative spirit, it is nevertheless true that some of its inspiration is drawn directly from the Bronze Age World.

5. **The interior of the so-called Treasury of Atreus, Mycenae.** *c.* 1400 BC. diam. 48 ft. (14.6 m.) × h. 44 ft. (13.4 m.). This is the largest and best preserved of the Tholos tombs of Mycenae.

The Beginnings of Greek Art

THE DARK AGES

The Greek Dark Ages are now not so dark. There is no history, it is true; only a vague memory in later times of the catastrophes that brought about the end of the Mycenaean world. But archaeology, in so far as it can, is slowly bridging the gap between the downfall of the Mycenaean world and the emergence into history of the Greek city-states in the 7th century BC. Greek tradition associated the collapse of the Mycenaeans with an invasion of new Greek-speaking people, the Dorians, who settled in and dominated several of the Mycenaean centres, bringing with them, it seems, the use of iron, different burial customs, and a different way of life. The Dorian invasion not only established the historical pattern of settlement in mainland Greece, but had as one of its effects the migration of Greek settlers to the islands and the Asiatic coast of Turkey, which is the basis of the eastern Greek world. The evidence of archaeology now throws light on the course of this migration, and the slow recovery of prosperity that made possible the achievements of the historical Greeks.

THE EMERGENCE OF A NEW ART

The Dorian invasion does not seem to have provided any new artistic stimulus, and it was in Athens, which claimed to have been untouched by the invasion, that the emergence of a new artistic spirit in the 11th century can be most clearly seen. It comes as a great surprise to those who think of Greek art in the terms of its 5th-century achievements, that it begins with a completely abstract phase in which the human figure and the world of nature have no place. In this age of poverty and obscurity, the only documents for the history of art are the painted pots which served both domestic and funerary purposes. The style of painting that succeeded the sub-Mycenaean is known as the proto-geometric, the earliest phase of a tradition of ornament based upon geometric patterns that prevailed until the end of the 8th century BC.

There is a world of difference between a sub-Mycenaean and a proto-geometric pot, between the decadent naturalism of the one and the strict formalism of the other. The difference is seen in the shapes of the pots (plate 22), which are much more precise in outline and have the various parts more clearly defined, in the symmetrical arrangement of the ornamental bands, and the accuracy with which the ornamental motifs—the compass-drawn concentric circles, the precise chequer patterns—are carried out. Certain Mycenaean elements survive in the pottery, but nevertheless, with the proto-geometric, art in Greece takes on a new direction and a completely new discipline. It is at first sight surprising that this non-representational phase should form the basis for the development of Greek art; but even in these humble beginnings the virtues of proportion, symmetry, clarity and precision, on which all its greatest achievements were founded, are clearly present.

THE GEOMETRIC STYLE

The proto-geometric style of pot-painting seems to have originated in Athens about 1000 BC, and Athens led the Greek world in art throughout the geometric phase. The development of the geometric style shows an increasing repertory of motifs—zigzags, lozenges, meanders—until in the late geometric of the 8th century BC the pot was covered overall with bands of ornament. Figures of any kind were slow to appear. There is a little horse, rather casually placed, on a proto-geometric pot of the 10th century, but it is not until the 8th century that humans and animals have a place of any importance in the pot-painters scheme of things. When the human figure does appear he is a strange creature, painted as a silhouette with the head shown in profile, and distinguished by a reserved area with a blob in it for the eye; the body is shown frontal in the form of a triangle; the arms are like match-sticks; and the legs appear in profile with rounded buttocks and strong calves. It hardly needs saying that the geometric painter is not attempting to represent what he sees, but he hardly ever leaves us in doubt as to what he means. He will draw all four wheels of a chariot seen in profile, because he knows that his chariot has four wheels whether they can be seen from his chosen viewpoint or not, and, on this basis, he can tackle quite complicated scenes, and make them understandable.

The vases of the so-called Dipylon style made in Athens in about 750 are the high water mark of geometric art. The biggest Dipylon vases—the one from which our detail on plate 23 is taken stands over 5 feet high—were placed above ground to mark the positions of tombs in the Dipylon cemetery at Athens, and they may be considered as the first real attempts at monumental art in early Greece. The figure compositions, though comparatively small in scale, have pride of place. The scene illustrated here is a typical one showing the dead man laid out on a bier surrounded by his family and mourners; an enormous chequered canopy frames the scene. Other vases of the same class have secondary friezes with processions of chariots and armed warriors, and some contemporary vases depict battle scenes of various kinds, inspired probably by the subject matter of Greek epic poetry. If so, they stand at the head of the tradition of mythological representation in Greek art, which was to be its main source of inspiration, and they bring us out of the Dark Ages into the realm of Greek history.

THE ORIGINS OF GREEK SCULPTURE

The documents for the history of sculpture during this period are much more scanty than those for painting. Clearly, there was no monumental sculpture of any kind during the Dark Ages, but there was a considerable output of small-scale work in bronze and terracotta in many places. In Crete, human and animal bronzes were made in a decadent Minoan style long after the collapse of Minoan civilisation. Elsewhere primitive figures with hardly a definable style continued to be made. By the 8th century a figure style corresponding closely to the geometric formula seen on pottery became fairly widespread. Little bronze horses with short cylindrical bodies, almost cylindrical heads, long legs and strongly developed fore- and hindquarters are the three-dimensional counterparts of the painted figures. Human beings were also represented in the clear-cut geometric formula. The bronze group of a man and a centaur, perhaps Herakles and Nessos (plate 24), in the Metropolitan Museum, New York, was made about 750 BC. The bronze figure of Apollo in Boston (plate 29), which seems to be a Boeotian work of about 700, shows the fully developed geometric scheme for the human figure with long triangular face and large eyes, long neck, triangular body and strongly developed thighs. The inscription reveals that the statuette was dedicated to the god Apollo, by a certain Mantiklos. In these minor works of sculpture Greek artists found their first simple, straightforward formula for the representation of human and animal figures, which could serve as the basis for future development.

EARLY GREEK BUILDINGS

As in painting and sculpture, so in architecture, the basis of the Greek styles was laid in the Dark Ages. We have much less to go on here than in the other arts. 'The surviving buildings of the Dark Age', says A. W. Lawrence, 'are few in number and of deplorable quality'. It is possible, however, to follow some of the steps by which the most characteristic of Greek buildings, the temple, took on the shape it was to have in later times. There had been no temples in the Bronze Age, and we do not know when they began to be built. The Olympian religion of the Greeks, which contains both Bronze Age and later elements, conceived its gods in human form. Very early on they must have been represented by cult-images of some kind, and these cult-images required to be properly housed; so it was natural that the earliest temples should take the form of houses. In the Dark Ages houses might be circular, elliptical or rectangular and, no doubt, many of the earliest temples assumed these various forms. But the rectangular shape soon predominated. One of the earliest surviving temples, at Thermon in Aetolia, is designed on the plan of a Mycenaean megaron; it would have been built of mudbricks with a ridged timber roof. A model of a simple temple with a porch and high-pitched roof has survived from the end of the geometric period. A vital development took place when colonnades were put round the main temple building, thus creating the essential form of later Greek temples, and this may have happened as early as 750 BC; the first temple of Hera at Samos, which belongs to this period, is the earliest known example. Certainly, by the early 7th century the Greek temple, constructed of mud brick and wood, had assumed its essential form, and the way was open for the development of the Greek orders of stone architecture.

THE GREEKS AND THE EAST

In architecture, painting and sculpture the Dark Ages, which saw the slow revival of prosperity in Greece, laid the foundations of the development of Greek art. By 750, when the geometric style reached its acme in Athens, the Greek city-states were beginning to plant their first colonies abroad, trade with the eastern Mediterranean was reopened, and Greek art was open to new ideas derived from imitation of imported objects and things seen by the Greeks abroad. At the same time, renewed prosperity made possible big projects in architecture and sculpture. The new ideas came predominantly from the eastern Mediterranean through a variety of different sources; from the neighbours of the Greeks in Anatolia, through Phoenician traders, from direct Greek contacts in Egypt and in many other ways. These ideas did not change the fundamental character of Greek art; the reception of foreign ideas was accompanied by a flair, amounting to genius, for adapting them into the living and developing tradition.

The oriental influence is first seen in pottery with the introduction of new decorative elements, a new repertory of formal and naturalistic patterns and a whole new world of strange animals, real and fantastic (plate 26). There is no sharp break with the geometric figure-style; what we see is a slow relaxing of the strict principles of geometric painting with the severe silhouette giving place to some outline drawing and the bodily forms becoming more rounded. On the Athenian vase, illustrated in plate 27, which dates from around 700 BC, the lions are inspired by oriental sources, but the chief interest lies in the treatment of the chariot scene above; the horses move more naturally than geometric horses, and instead of the odd combinations of frontal view and profile that characterise the pure geometric figure style, the figures are shown consistently in profile. On this vase the prominence given to the figure scenes is evidence of the general development of the taste for figure painting during the period.

In the 7th century, many centres of the Greek world were making fine pottery influenced by the newly discovered oriental repertory. On the mainland, at Corinth, the leader of the commercial states of Greece, which had already been producing a refined type of geometric pottery without figures, there was developed a style which at first adopted horizontal bands of real and imaginary animals (plate 25), and soon added figure compositions, including mythological scenes, to its sources of inspiration. It was the Corinthian painters who developed the black-figure technique which was to dominate Greek pot-painting until the late 6th century. In this technique the figures are painted in dark silhouette on the natural colour of the clay; details of the anatomy, which increasingly interest the painter, are shown by engraved lines, and pure silhouette is also relieved by a few added colours, among them white and purple. The most famous of 7th-century Corinthian vases is the so-called Chigi Jug in the Villa Giulia Museum, Rome, which was found in Etruria. The body of this vessel is dec-

6. **The Kore of Auxerre.** *c.* 640 BC.
Limestone. h. 25½ in. (65 cm.).
Louvre, Paris. Small figure of a young
woman, in the so-called Daedalic style,
probably made as a votive offering.

orated with horizontal bands of figured ornament showing
battle and hunting scenes, a procession of chariots, and a
mythological subject — the Judgment of Paris. The painted
pots made at this time in the eastern Greek cities are often
attractively colourful. One of the best known groups, which
was made in Rhodes, is generally decorated with bands of
animal figures and ornament over a white slip that covers
the body of the vessel.

THE BEGINNINGS OF MONUMENTAL SCULPTURE

The problem of the origins of monumental sculpture in
Greece is a very vexed one. The only works of sculpture
surviving from the Dark Ages are small bronzes and terracottas. There is some evidence from later Greek tradition
that the earliest cult-images were of wood, but of their appearance there is very little to be said. The historical reasons for the rise of monumental sculpture in the 7th century
are clear enough; prosperity gave the opportunity for ex-
pensive projects, and in Egypt, and elsewhere in the Orient,
the Greeks saw temples and statues of men and gods which
could serve as models to imitate. By the middle of the 7th
century, certainly, the Greeks were making use of their fine
local sources of stone and marble to carve big figures, both
cult-images and statues of men.

Greek art, beginning from a purely non-representational
approach, had, by the 8th century, developed the geometric formulae for human and animal figures. The search
for an ideal scheme of human, and divine, form now found
inspiration in the achievements of Egyptian art. Greek
sculpture of the 7th century is associated with the name of
the mythical Daedalus of Crete, who in legend was the
first Greek sculptor. The 'Daedalic' style is widespread in
the 7th century on the Greek mainland and in the islands.
The narrow-waisted broad shouldered form of the male
figure still owes something to the geometric 'canon', but
the oriental elements are clear in the coiffure which is often
a version of an Egyptian wig, and in the poses of the figures.
The figure of a girl illustrated in figure 6 is a 'Daedalic'
work of about 640 BC. Her long triangular face and wig-like
headdress, the simplicity of the forms beneath her long
garment, are typical of the style. Her dress is decorated
with engraving, and was once richly coloured, as was all
archaic sculpture.

By the end of the 7th century, Greek artists had developed
a form of standing male figure which is completely free of
geometric conventions, and, although strongly influenced
by oriental models, is properly their own. Figure 7 represents an over life-size marble statue dedicated at the
sanctuary of Poseidon on Cape Sunium, at the south-
eastern tip of Attica. It illustrates perfectly the simple archaic 'canon' of male figure sculpture. The figure stands
erect and strictly frontal with his left leg advanced, his arms
tense at his sides with fists clenched. Details are represented
with strength and simplicity. The eyes are big and almond-
shaped, the ears large and so carved as to form a kind of
decorative adjunct; the essential parts of the body are

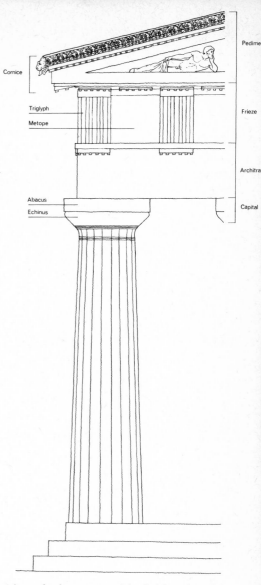

7. **Kouros from Sunion.** *c.* 600 BC. Marble. h. 10 ft. (3.05 m.). National Museum, Athens. Found in a pit near the temple of Poseidon at Sunion, together with remains of other statues. The figure has been put together from fragments. Its left arm is modern.

C. The Doric Order.

clearly defined and subject to an established canon of proportions, while muscles and bones form surface patterns on the marble. The work already has those qualities of grandeur and proportion which characterise all the best Greek sculpture throughout its history. Female figures of the same period are always represented clothed, and are not subjected to a single rigid scheme. In early female statues the lower part of the body beneath the clothes may be shown flat and board-like, or cylindrical, with the folds of the garment indicated by vertical lines, but there is the same simplicity and monumental quality, and the same attempt to find a clear and direct formula.

EARLY HISTORY OF GREEK ARCHITECTURE

The development of architecture during the 7th century was rapid. The basic Greek temple form, as has been seen, had been created during the 'Dark Ages', but it was not until the 7th century that the Greek 'Orders of Architecture' began to take shape. Nothing illustrates better the characteristic Greek search for an ideal form to refine and perfect, than the Doric style of architecture. Its origins lie in the wooden forms of the earliest Greek architecture, as a brief look at its essential elements will show (plate 38). The columns rise without a base from the floor of the building, and are vertically fluted throughout their length; the capitals which surmount them consist of a spreading convex

moulding (the *echinus*), and a low square block (the *abacus*). The plain *architrave* is made up of a series of rectangular lintel blocks spanning between the columns; above that comes the frieze, which is divided up into a series of panels *(metopes)* by projecting blocks, each having three vertical bands separated by grooves *(triglyphs)*. The crowning member is the cornice, a continuous projecting stone eave, downward tilting on its underside and adorned with rectangular slabs carrying projecting pegs. Many of these features have a direct origin in wooden prototypes. The triglyphs of the frieze derive from decorative treatment of the ends of the structural roof beams, and there is a similar explanation for the detail on the underside of the cornice; the column and its capital must have been based on wooden originals.

The Doric order was firmly established by about 600 BC, and thereafter undergoes remarkably little change except in the direction of increasing refinement. The shape of the capitals (see plate 38), the proportions of the various parts, develop and change, but the essential form remains the same. The Temple of Hera at Olympia, built about 600 BC, has a fully developed temple plan with a rectangular *cella*, colonnaded porches at either end, a surrounding colonnade, a pitched roof creating the triangular space *(pediment)* between the horizontal and raking cornices, and a standard classical arrangement of six columns along the

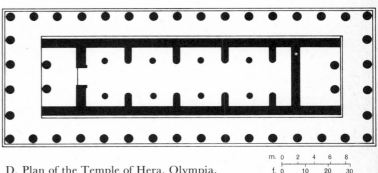

D. Plan of the Temple of Hera, Olympia.

m. 0 2 4 6 8
f. 0 10 20 30

8. **Medusa and her son Chrysaor.**
Early 6th century BC. Marble. h. 10¼ ft.
(3.15 m.). Museum of Corfu, Greece.
The central group of the east pediment
of the Temple of Artemis at Corcyra.

front. This particular temple was originally built of wood,
but there were already stone temples in the middle of the
7th century.

In contrast with the Doric, the second of the two great
orders of Greek architecture, the Ionic, which was especially favoured by the city-states of Asiatic Greece, did not
achieve a canonical form at this period, not, indeed, until
the later part of the 5th century BC. Its origins are more
obscure; the early forms of the Ionic capital, with its characteristic volutes, admit of considerable variations, and the
details of the superstructure are different from place to
place. But from the very beginning, the two orders are
clearly distinguished; the columns of the Ionic have pro-
filed bases, and the system of fluting is quite different. The
architrave is stepped not plain, and the cornice is marked
by a range of close-set projecting blocks *(dentils)* below the
main projection. Sometimes a plain continuous frieze is introduced, but not at first in association with dentils. The
early Ionic temples of Asiatic Greece are more ambitious
and grander in scale than the Doric; we see this most clearly
in the plans of the 6th-century temple at Samos, and of the
enormous temple of Artemis at Ephesus put up about
560 BC. In both there was a double row of huge columns
surrounding the main building, and in scale these early
Ionic temples were hardly ever surpassed in later Greek
building.

THE DECORATION OF BUILDINGS

The development of the standard forms of Greek temples
in the 7th century give rise to new classes of sculpture and
painting concerned with their decoration. Some fragments
of sculpture in the Daedalic style of about 640, found on the
site of a temple on the Acropolis of Mycenae, seem to be
the earliest examples of sculpture serving to decorate the
metopes of a Doric frieze. If an early temple was built of
wood the metopes would be made of painted terracotta,
and there are fragments of terracotta metopes, dating from
the second half of the 7th century, from a temple dedicated
to Apollo at Thermon in Aetolia. They are, in fact, the
earliest examples of monumental painting that have survived from archaic Greece; their style is Corinthian, closely
related to that of contemporary vases. One of the finest
fragments shows a seated woman, a fine outline drawing
with washes of colour—white for face and arms, black for
hair, and purple for the dress. Essentially the same technique as that of the vase-painters is used for this work on a
larger scale.

The triangular space of the temple pediment cried out
for some decorative treatment. The earliest surviving example of pedimental sculpture, dating from the early 6th
century BC, comes from the temple of Artemis in the Corinthian colony of Corcyra (Corfu). The solution of the difficult problem of the slope of the pediment is not particularly

E. Reconstruction of the pediment of the Temple of Artemis at
Corcyra.

successful, but the giant Gorgon in the centre of the pediment (figure 8) is a magnificent creation. She is depicted
in the kneeling pose which serves to represent a running
action, and she is flanked by two heraldic lion-panthers;
the rest of the triangular space is taken up with smaller
figures: her sons Chrysaor and Pegasus beside her and figure
groups near the corners. Some fine fragments of early
pedimental compositions have also been found in the
debris of the Persian sack of the Acropolis of Athens; the
group of frightening scale and character, showing a lioness
attacking a bull (plate 31), was made about 600 BC, and
belongs to a world where monsters and exotic creatures still
have power to terrify men. This sculpture associated with
buildings posed difficult problems in the grouping of
figures, which gave a great impetus to the development of
Greek figure-sculpture.

THE ART OF THE SIXTH CENTURY

By 600 BC the subject-matter of Greek painting and sculpture, and the standard forms of temple architecture, were
fully established. The period of oriental influences was
over, and Greek art began to go its own way. Although
there are almost no surviving examples of monumental
painting from the 6th century, many painted vases, some
of the highest quality, have come down to us; there is a
body of original sculpture much larger than for any other
period of Greek art. Temples and other buildings have
either survived to the present day or are well-known from
the results of excavations. The 6th century is an age of great
achievement in art, as in almost every other branch of life.
Artists were always searching for new ideas and increasing
their understanding of the problems of representational art.
Ignorance is not shortcoming, and what they do, they do
superlatively well; some of their work has a clarity and a
nobility that is scarcely ever surpassed in the history of art.

ATHENIAN VASE-PAINTING

We may begin to consider the last phase of archaic Greek
art with the paintings on pottery made in Athens. The pots
of this time are decorated in the black-figure technique,
black painted silhouette against the rich red of the fired
clay, with internal details of the figures drawn with incised
line and a few added colours, especially white and purple.
It is a technique that is exclusive to the pot-painter; on
wall-paintings or panel pictures made in the same period
we should probably find that, though the same principles
of outline drawing filled with colour prevailed there too,
the artist's palette was a much larger one, comparable to
that used in the colouring of sculpture during the time. But
the vases give a good idea of the advances made in representational art during the 6th century.

The vase illustrated in plate 28 is one of the latest examples of enormous funerary vases in the tradition of the
Dipylon vase (plate 23), the work of a pot-painter who was
active in Athens around 600 BC, and who painted in a big
style appropriate to the scale of the pots. On the neck of the
vessel, in a panel, appears the episode of the hero Herakles
killing the Centaur Nessos, a favourite scene from legend;
our detail (plate 28) shows one of the two hideous sisters of
Medusa, who appear on the body of the vase, rushing from
the scene of her decapitation. The kneeling pose, with the
legs in profile, which is the early convention for running
figures, is still used here, and the painter has swung the
enormous heads and the upper parts of the bodies frontally,
to reveal their terrifying appearance. The Nessos painter,
so named after the scene he painted on this vase, is, within
the limits of his technique, a brilliant and powerful illustrator.

The black-figure style in Athens comes to full fruition
around 560 BC, when the tyrant Pisistratus was in power in
the city. His patronage of the arts inspired great achieve-

(Continued on page 57)

22. **Proto-geometric vase.** *c*. 1000 BC.
Pottery. h. 13¾ in. (34 cm.). British
Museum, London. The vase is very simply
decorated in the style apparently created
in Athens during the 11th century BC.
The chequer pattern on the upper part of
the body is a typical motif; the wavy band
on the main frieze is perhaps a survival
from the Mycenaean decorative tradition.

23. (left). **A funeral scene.** 8th century BC. Pottery. h. (of vase) 5 ft. 1 in. (1.55 m.) National Museum, Athens. This detail is from a very large painted vase found in the Dipylon cemetery at Athens, where it served to mark a tomb. The scene shows the dead man on a bier, lying in state beneath a chequered canopy, attended by mourners. It is one of the finest surviving examples of geometric vase-painting.

24. (below). **Man and Centaur.** 8th century BC. Bronze. h. 4½ in. (11.4 cm.). Metropolitan Museum of Art, New York. Gift of J. Pierpont Morgan, 1917. This little group has been interpreted as Herakles killing the Centaur Nessos. The man apparently held a sword in his right hand but there is little suggestion of any violent action in the composition. The forms of man and beast are typical of geometric sculpture in Greece during the 8th century—triangular body, narrow waist, bulging thighs and a flat face. There was no large-scale sculpture in this period but many such figures of men and animals and a few groups like this.

29. (left). **The Mantiklos Apollo.** Early 7th century. Bronze. h. 8 in. (20 cm.). Museum of Fine Arts, Boston. Statuette of the god Apollo from Thebes in Boeotia. The forms of the body are those established during the geometric period for the representation of the human form. The god wore a headdress and probably carried a bow in his left hand. On the thighs is an inscription saying that Mantiklos dedicated the figure to the god Apollo.

30. (right). **Detail of storage jar from Thebes.** *c.* 700 BC. Pottery. h. (of vase) 4 ft. 1¼ in. (1.25 m.). National Museum, Athens. Detail of a big amphora decorated with relief-ornament found in a tomb near Thebes. The detail shows the figure of a goddess, the Potnia Theron or Mistress of the Animals, who is accompanied here by two smaller human figures and flanked by two standing lions.

31. (above). **Lioness attacking a bull.** *c.* 600 BC. Painted limestone. approx. h. 5 ft. 7 in. (1.70 m.). Acropolis Museum, Athens. This powerful sculpture comes from the pediment of a building on the Acropolis. The complete group probably showed two lions, one on either side of the pediment, and a bull in the centre. The figures have been restored from many small fragments found in excavations.

32. **The three-bodied Monster.** *c.* 570 BC. Limestone. l. 11 ft. 4 in. (3.40 m.). Acropolis Museum, Athens. Part of a pediment from a temple on the Acropolis at Athens, destroyed in the Persian sack of 480 BC. The left half of the pediment showed Herakles wrestling with Triton and the right, illustrated here, a weird three-bodied monster with a tail in the form of twisted snakes. Much of the ancient paint still survives on the carving. The pediment is often called the 'Blue-beard pediment' because hair and beards of the creature are painted dark blue.

33. (left). **Kore No. 679.** *c.* 530 BC.
Marble. h. 4 ft. (1.21 m.). Acropolis
Museum, Athens. The 'Peplos Kore' is
one of the best-known of the series of
figures of maidens (*korai*) dedicated on the
Acropolis of Athens in the 6th century
and destroyed by the Persians. The painting on this figure, as on others of the
series, is fairly well preserved. The clothes
she wears are the sleeveless Doric *peplos*
of heavy material over a lighter garment

with sleeves (*chiton*). Her gently smiling
face, typical of archaic sculpture in Greece,
has wonderful life and charm and, for all
the apparent simplicity of the figure,
the forms of the body beneath the drapery
are suggested with consummate skill.

34. (right). **Bronze Kouros from
Piraeus.** *c.* 530 BC. Bronze. h. 6 ft. 3 in.
(1.90 m.). National Museum, Athens.
This statue was found by workmen digging
a drain in 1959 at Piraeus, the port of
Athens. It is the earliest large hollow cast
bronze figure which has survived from the
Greek world and belongs to a period
when the technique had not long been
discovered. It probably represents the
god Apollo, who was shown holding a
bow in his left hand.

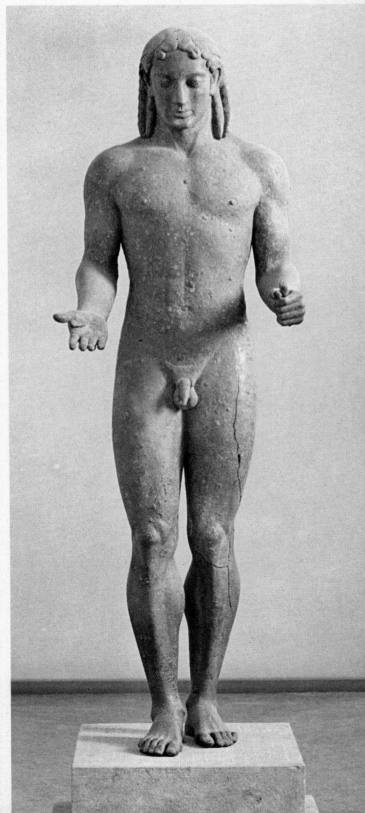

35. (right). **Banqueter.** Late 6th century BC. Bronze. l. 4 in. (10 cm.). British Museum, London. This statuette, perhaps from the rim of a large bowl, is said to have been found at Dodona, the sanctuary of Zeus in Epirus.

36. (left). **The Rampin Horseman.** c. 550 BC. Marble. h. 3 ft. 7½ in. (1.10 m.). Acropolis Museum, Athens. This statue of a horse and rider was one of the dedications on the Acropolis of Athens destroyed by the Persians under Xerxes in 480 BC. To judge from the oak wreath he wears, the rider was the victor of a horse race. It is believed to be an earlier work of the sculptor who carved the 'Peplos Kore' (plate 33). The head is a cast of the so-called Rampin head in the Louvre, which gives its name to the whole group.

37. (right). **Exekias. Attic black-figure vase.** c. 530 BC. Pottery. h. 16¼ in. (41 cm.). British Museum, London. This amphora, by one of the finest black-figure painters of Athens, showing Achilles slaying Penthesilea, is a perfect example of the technique consisting of black silhouette with engraved detail and white and purple paint added for some details. On the other side of the vase Dionysos appears with his son Oinopion.

38. (above). **The 'Temple of Neptune' at Paestum** (mid-5th century BC) and part of the so-called Basilica (mid-6th century) in the foreground. The view of these two temples shows something of the development of Doric architecture from the archaic to the classical period. The columns of the earlier building taper more markedly towards the top and the *echinus* of the capital is flatter and more spreading.

39. **Part of the frieze of the Siphnian Treasury, Delphi.** Archeological Museum, Delphi. *c.* 525 BC. Marble. h. 2 ft. 2 in. (66 cm.). The frieze ran round the whole building, and more than half of it still survives. The subjects on the west and south sides were the Judgment of Paris and the Rape of the Leucippids; on the east and north, scenes from the Trojan War and Battle of Gods and Giants. The detail shown here is part of the Gods and Giants frieze; Cybele is in her chariot drawn by lions, Herakles in the background fights with a giant.

40. (left). **Aristokles. The Stele of Aristion.** Late 6th century BC. Marble. h. 8 ft. (2.4 m.). National Museum, Athens. Aristion appears in military dress, wearing breastplate, greaves and helmet; the top of the gravestone was once crowned by a palmette. The figure is carved in low relief; of the rich painting the red on the hair and beard is best preserved. Found near Velanidesa in Attica. An inscription gives the name of the sculptor.

41, 42. (right and below). **The crater of Vix and detail showing frieze.** *c.* 525 BC. Bronze. h. 5 ft. 4 in. (1.64 m.). Museum at Châtillon-sur-Seine. This fine mixing-bowl was found in 1953 at Vix near Châtillon-sur-Seine (Côte d'Or) in a rich chariot burial of the late Hallstatt period. The vessel is made of hammered bronze decorated with cast appliqué figures on the neck and equipped with elaborate cast handles. The frieze on the neck, of which a detail is shown here, depicts four-horse chariots and soldiers (*hoplites*). This is one of the finest surviving Greek bronze vessels and its presence at Vix illustrates the wide extent of Greek trade north of the Alps.

43, 44. (opposite). **The Andokides Painter. Bilingual amphora** (both sides). Late 6th century BC. Pottery. h. 21 in. (53.5 cm.). Antikensammlungen, Munich. The same scene (with variations) of Herakles banqueting on Olympus appears on both sides of the vase, once in the red-figure technique and once in black-figure. In the late 6th century, when the red-figure technique was coming into fashion, a number of vases were painted making use of both techniques. A comparison of the two scenes illustrates the advantages of the red-figure technique over its predecessor.

ments in architecture, sculpture and painting. We see evidence for a building programme on the Acropolis comparable to that under Pericles in the 5th century. The Athens of Pisistratus was a cosmopolitan place; artists from all over the Greek world, including the Ionian cities, came to work there. The great advances in the art of painting are reflected in the vase pictures. The painters who made these luxury vessels often signed their works; others are not known by name, but their work on different vases can be recognised. Exekias, who painted the vase in the British Museum illustrated on plate 37, is perhaps the greatest black-figure vase painter of Athens. He has chosen for his subject here the popular episode of Achilles slaying Penthesilea, the queen of the Amazons, and he represents it at the moment when the hero has plunged his sword into the Amazon's body, as she desperately defends herself on one knee. The painter achieves the effect of life and movement by drawing without any of the tricks of foreshortening, and shows a remarkable ability to illustrate so dramatic a moment simply and directly. There are many other fine black-figure painters whose work is admired, but this painting by Exekias may justly stand for their achievements, for the exquisite quality of their draughtsmanship, and the powerful simplicity of their work.

BLACK-FIGURE AND RED-FIGURE

In the last quarter of the 6th century BC, the black-figure style gave way to a new technique, that of red-figure. Red-figure is, in simple terms, a reversal of black-figure. The pot-painter instead of painting his figures in black silhouette against the red clay, paints the background in black and leaves the figures in the natural colour of the clay. The advantages of the new technique are obvious; the black-figure painter has to incise the internal details of his figures. The red-figure painter can draw or paint them in line, and by this means has much greater opportunity to convey natural movement. The new technique appears at a time when the painters were becoming more and more concerned with the problems involved in creating an illusion of three-dimensionality in representing the human figure; whereas the black-figure painter generally showed his figures either strictly frontal or in profile, or awkwardly combined the two viewpoints, the red-figure painter wants to show twists of the body, suggest subtle movements, and introduce unusual views. Another technique of vase-painting, which was becoming increasingly popular in the late 6th century, allowed the use of a wider range of colours. This is the white-ground technique, in which the body of the vase is covered with a white slip, the design is drawn in outline and filled in with washes of colour—red, purple, brown and yellow, a range of colours that probably gives an idea of the palette of contemporary wall-painting.

At first, red-figure and black-figure were practised together, sometimes on the same vase. The vase by the Andokides painter illustrated in plates 43–44 has the same scene on both sides, one in red-figure and one in black-figure.

Very soon the more progressive artists have all turned to red-figure. In the last two decades of the 6th century the best red-figure painters delight in showing the human figure in different, complicated poses, and they begin to master the principles of foreshortening and anatomy in action. The work of Oltos on cups, and Euphronios on big vases, shows remarkable ability to suggest the solidity of three-dimensional form by pure line drawing.

SIXTH-CENTURY SCULPTURE

The development of Greek painting in the 6th century can only be studied with the aid of the vases, which, however fine their quality, are secondary sources; the major art of painting is almost unknown. In the case of sculpture, the primary documents themselves have survived. In 480 BC, when the Persians under Xerxes sacked the Acropolis of Athens, buildings and sculpture were destroyed, and, when Athens was reoccupied, these fragments were not restored but were used as rubble-filling in new walls and foundations; many of them have been excavated in a condition which, though fragmentary, is almost as fresh as the day they were cast down. Excavations in other parts of the Greek world have yielded many fine archaic sculptures and we can now appreciate the styles of the eastern cities and other centres of the Greek mainland. Apart from major works, small bronzes and work in other materials fill out the picture of archaic sculpture in the 6th century.

9. **Sphinx.** *c*. 550 BC. Marble. h. 21⅝ in. (55 cm.). Acropolis Museum, Athens. This figure of a sphinx, found on the Acropolis at Athens, was part of a votive offering.

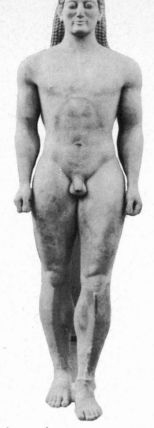

10. **Kouros.** *c.* 520 BC. h. 6 ft. 4 in. (1.94 m.). National Museum, Athens. Statue of a young man, whose name, according to an inscription, was Kroisos. Found at Anavyssos in Attica, in 1936.

THE 'KOUROS' AND 'KORE'

The development of sculpture in this period is a comparatively simple story. In figure-sculpture the ideal schemes of the nude *kouros* and the draped female *(kore)* hold the field until the early years of the 5th century. Decoration on buildings—pedimental sculpture, metopes, and friezes—provides the main inspiration for experiments with the posing and grouping of figures which, by the end of the century, have achieved such freedom, that they seem about to break with conventions and achieve a completely free range of expression. A major influence on the development of Greek sculpture was the discovery, in the first half of the century, of the technique of hollow-casting large bronze figures; the only surviving archaic bronze figure, the *kouros* recently found at the Piraeus and now in Athens (plate 34), has the same hard transitions as the marble figures of the period, as though the model from which it was cast had been carved in hard material. Modelling in clay, which is the basis of the bronze worker's technique, allowed greater freedom in composition, and bronze became the favourite medium of the great sculptors of the 5th century.

The sculptors of the 6th century were keenly interested in the problems of rendering the anatomy of the human figure, and although the archaic scheme and its conventions were not abandoned, the statues become more lifelike in face and figure. A work of the later 6th century (figure 10) shows how the four-square structure of the earlier figures has been relaxed, the forms are more rounded, less abrupt, the anatomical details represented more nearly as they are in nature. If we look at the fine grave relief of Aristion in the National Museum at Athens, one of the series of superb gravestones made for wealthy Athenians of the period, we can see how far the sculptors have progressed in this direction by the end of the century. It is a vivid and personal representation of a man, superbly modelled and subtle in detail (plate 40). It is, indeed, remarkable how 6th century sculptors can portray the individual; we see their ability most clearly in the series of archaic maidens in the Acropolis Museum, one of the finest of which is the figure illustrated in plate 33, a work of wonderful individuality and charm. She wears a Doric garment, the *peplos*, and is called the *Peplos Kore*. Most of her sisters on the Acropolis wear Ionian dress, on which the sculptor exercised his skill in rendering the contrast between the heavier folds of the cloak *(himation)*, and the soft material of the undergarment *(chiton)*. The sculptors of the 6th century were also tackling many new poses and compositions in the round. The figure illustrated in plate 36 is part of an equestrian statue dedicated on the Acropolis in about 540 BC; the remains of the horse and body of the rider are in the Acropolis Museum at Athens, and the head, of which a cast is shown in the picture, is in the Louvre. It seems to be a work of the same sculptor who carved the *Peplos Kore*.

The little bronze figure of a reclining banqueter (plate 35), in the British Museum, is an exquisite piece, which illustrates the high standard of craftsmanship in small-scale work. On a similar scale we may compare with it the superb detail of the procession of chariots on the well-known crater of Vix, a big bronze vase found in a chieftain's tomb in central France, and dating from the late 6th century BC (plates 41 & 42). By this time Greek sculptors have acquired a wonderful mastery in representing the essential forms of human and animal alike. The marble figure of a horse in the Acropolis Museum at Athens may stand for their skill in rendering animal forms; the piece is archaic in its firmness and simplification of anatomical detail, but we shall not have again in Greek art a more convincing representation of the animal (figure 16).

IONIAN GREECE

In this brief discussion of archaic sculpture the examples have been mostly drawn from Attica, but there are other important regional styles which must not be entirely ignored here. The statue of a man from Samos, shown in figure 11, may perhaps serve to illustrate some of the more obvious differences between the sculpture of the mainland and that of Ionia. The draped male figure is very rare in mainland Greece, but seems to have been common in Ionia. It also seems that the more fleshy type of male was respected, or at least frequently represented, by the sculptors; the man from Samos provides a marked contrast with the more compact ideal of Attic sculptors and those of the mainland in general.

ARCHITECTURAL SCULPTURE IN THE SIXTH CENTURY

We shall not deal in this chapter with the further development of architectural forms, except in so far as it affects the development of sculpture. We have already seen that in the 7th century a rich sculptural decoration began to be ap-

11. **Man from Samos.** *c.* 550 BC. Marble. h. 6¼ ft. (1.90 m.). Statues of draped male figures were very rare in mainland Greece, but more common in the cities of Ionia.

12. **Herakles.** *c.* 490 BC. Marble. h. 3 ft. 3 in. (1 m.). Antikensammlungen, Munich. Figure of Herakles drawing his bow, from the east pediment of the so-called Temple of Aphaia, at Aegina, was part of a composition depicting a battle in the Trojan War. (see figure F). This and other figures of the pediment were restored by the sculptor Thorwaldsen.

plied to buildings, and in the following century this decoration provided one of the most important fields for the development of sculptural styles. Fragments of 6th-century buildings from the Acropolis at Athens illustrate the progress in solving the problems of pedimental composition. Part of the famous 'bluebeard' pediment from a building of about 560 BC is illustrated in plate 32; here the sculptor has chosen a subject particularly appropriate to the difficult shape of the pediment, a weird and wonderful creation of a three-headed monster with a serpent's body filling the corner. A group depicting Herakles fighting Triton occupied the corresponding place on the other side of the pediment. There is a fine decorative use of colour, dark blue for the creature's beard and hair, deep red for the snakes and reddy-yellow on the skin. He is hardly a fierce beast but a friendly, almost amiable monster.

By the end of the century sculptors had mastered the problems of combining figures on the same scale into a single pedimental composition. The figure of Herakles illustrated in figure 12 comes from the east pediment of the Temple of Aphaia at Aegina, designed about 490 BC. The subject was a battle before Troy, in which mythical Aeginetan heroes took part; the centre of the pediment was dominated by the standing figure of the goddess Athena, while the fighting figures—striding forwards and backwards, kneeling, falling and fallen—are skilfully arranged in different poses to fill the triangular space. There is a fine freedom and variety in the representation of the figures. An example of early metope composition (figure 13) comes from a temple at Selinus, in Sicily, one of the Greek colonial cities which saw a great deal of important building activity in the 6th century. This composition of Perseus killing Medusa is stiff and somewhat retarded in style for its period, but it shows well the kind of composition that the

F. Reconstruction of the east pediment of the Temple of Aphaia at Aegina.

13. Perseus and Medusa. *c.* 550–540 BC. Marble. h. 4 ft. 10 in. (1.47 m.). Museo Nazionale, Palermo. Perseus, with Athena in attendance, is cutting off the head of Medusa; one of the metopes from the temple, known as temple C, at Selinus, in Sicily.

14. Young men playing a ball-game. *c.* 510 BC. Marble. h. 13 in. (32 cm.). National Museum, Athens. One side of a marble statue base found in the Dipylon cemetery at Athens, with reliefs showing a group of athletes playing a ball-game.

Greeks found appropriate for the metopes of the Doric frieze. The Ionic order included the continuous sculptured frieze. We have no examples of the period from large buildings, but one of the finest works of archaic relief sculpture comes from an exquisite little Ionic building at Delphi erected by the wealthy Cycladic island of Siphnos about 525 BC. This building, one of the Treasuries put up by Greek cities at the main pan-Hellenic sanctuaries, was a little rectangular structure with two standing figures of maidens *(caryatids)* taking the place of columns to support the entablature of the porch. A continuous frieze ran all round the building representing various subjects, including battles of gods and giants. Plate 39 shows part of the battle frieze on the north side, where the goddess Cybele appears in her chariot drawn by lions, one of whom is attacking a helmeted giant. The background of the frieze was painted in blue and the figures in bright colours. The sculptor shows a remarkable skill in rendering the most minute detail and the subtleties of texture and form, and he makes a convincing attempt to create an illusion of spatial depth by means of relief height, the overlapping of figures, and the clever use of foreshortenings.

THE ACHIEVEMENT OF ARCHAIC GREEK ART

We may now attempt to summarise the achievements of Greek artists in the long period from the end of the Mycenaean world to the beginning of the 5th century. When the Greek artist, after the first purely non-representational phase of art, begins to be interested in the human figure, he looks for and finds a simple, almost childlike, formula. Almost as soon as it is devised, the formula is used for representing quite complicated narrative scenes derived from a rich mythology, which continues to be the subject-matter of much of classical art throughout its history. At the same time the Greeks begin their search for ideal form to represent gods and men. In the period of oriental influences they found an ideal for monumental sculpture in Egyptian art, not because it was the only art available as a model, but because it was sympathetic to their own aims and ideals. But the Greeks, and herein lies the difference between their art and what had gone before, were not content to accept this form as absolute, but developed it by constant reference to what they saw in nature. It is dangerous to look too closely into the causes of this development—why it should have been made in Greece and not elsewhere—but two factors are certainly of prime importance. Firstly the Greeks wished to represent their vivid mythological and epic tradition by an equally vivid narrative art; secondly, they, more than other peoples, found the inspiration for their ideals in human nature in which they fervently believed.

By the beginning of the 5th century, neither sculptors nor painters had achieved the complete break with archaic conventions. Painting, in so far as we can judge from the vases, was still outline drawing with flat washes in a limited range of colour, shading was not attempted, nor was the painter yet able to show a figure with absolute consistency from his chosen viewpoint. A frontal eye appears in a profile head; the principles of foreshortening are not yet fully understood. Sculpture, especially relief-sculpture, is rather more ambitious; the ball-players on one side of the well-known statue base in the National Museum at Athens (figure 14) show how close artists, inspired by the cult of athletics, were getting to a complete understanding of human anatomy in action. In architecture, the forms which were to be still further refined and perfected in the 5th century had been brought into being, and already have some outstanding achievements behind them. In all branches of art the scene is set for what the Greeks are to achieve in the great period of their history.

The Art of the City-States

In 490, and again in 480 BC, the Persians, who had subdued the Greek cities of Asia Minor, attempted to bring those of mainland Greece under their sway. The defeat of the Persian invasions inaugurated the greatest period in the history of the Greek city-states; it brought economic prosperity, self-confidence in their institutions and way of life, rich achievement in every branch of the arts. In the years that followed, Athens emerged as the leader of the Greek states against the Persian threat. She converted a league of defence into an empire and, under the leadership of Pericles, made herself great. The power of Athens, achieved against strong opposition from Sparta and other states of Greece, lasted until the Peloponnesian War. That war did more than destroy the power of Athens: it undermined the whole system of city-state organisation, weakening their strength and breaking down their faith in themselves and their way of life. After it, they maintained their independence until the middle of the 4th century, when they succumbed at last to the power of Macedon under Philip and his son, Alexander the Great. Throughout this great period of history, painters, sculptors and architects, devoting their talents to the service of the city-states, laid the foundation of European art.

THE REVOLUTION IN GREEK ART

It is customary to speak of a revolution in Greek art as having taken place in the early years of the 5th century, but it is not easy to understand its character and importance. We have seen how the archaic *kouros* type had been brought increasingly close to nature, how sculptors, especially those working on reliefs and the decoration of buildings, had made successful attempts to convey difficult action poses with accuracy and vitality. This steady development might be thought to lead on inevitably to the complete abandonment of the archaic formulae. But there is, nevertheless, a vital step to be taken and, so far as we know, it was not taken until the early years of the 5th century, when the sculptors, with their thorough understanding of the human form, felt able to abandon completely the traditional, almost magical, statuary-types of the standing male and female figures which had long served to represent both gods and humans.

It is difficult to fix this revolutionary step in time. There is a hint of change in the well-known bronze *Apollo of Piombino* in the Louvre, a work of about 490 BC, but the slight relaxing of the frontal pose is not fully expressed in the forms of the body. The complete break has been made by the sculptor of the so-called *Kritian Boy* (plate 46), a statue found in the Persian debris on the Acropolis, which was probably made just before 480 BC. This figure, 'the first beautiful nude in art', as Sir Kenneth Clark has called it, belongs to a different world from the archaic *kouros*. He no longer stands four-square and frontal with the weight of the body distributed evenly on two stiff legs; instead the weight is taken on the left leg while the right is drawn back and bent at the knee. There is movement in the body, with

one hip raised above the other, and the head is turned gently to the right. The face, too, is different, not only in structure but in expression; the keen, smiling archaic face has given place to a gently pensive and serious look that we associate with the artists of the 5th century. The *Kritian Boy* seems to set Greek sculpture on a new path: the search for an ideal of human and divine beauty, grounded in nature but disciplined by perfection of symmetry, proportion and balance. To this ideal Polykleitos, the great Argive sculptor, was to devote the greater part of his life and work in the second half of the 5th century.

THE GREAT ARTIST OF THE FIFTH CENTURY

If the fundamental break with the archaic world had already taken place before the Persian Wars, the Greek victories undoubtedly set the seal upon it and created the opportunity for the rapid development of the new tradition. It is not easy to follow this development in what has survived. The 5th century is an age of great names in sculpture and painting, but almost none of their work has come down to us. The great sculptors of the period, such as Myron and Polykleitos, worked mainly in bronze, and we know their masterpieces only from the copies that were made of them in Roman times. The work of the great painters, such as Polygnotus, is completely lost, and there are no copies; all we have are reflections of their style and technique in the work of contemporary vase-painters, and some information about them from second-hand literary sources. The monuments of architecture are better known, and the surviving buildings also provide a body of sculpture which is not only primary material for the development of the art, but sometimes gives evidence for the style of the great sculptors who were concerned with their decoration. From these various sources we know something of what the great artists achieved, though we have very little direct knowledge of their work.

THE TEMPLE OF ZEUS AT OLYMPIA

The sculptures from the great temple of Zeus at Olympia, begun about 470 and finished in 456 BC, give a starting point for the study of Greek sculpture in the years following the Persian Wars. Both pediments of this Doric temple were filled with sculptural compositions—on the west, a wild scene of fighting between the Lapiths and the Centaurs at the wedding feast of Peirithoos, and, on the east, a scene of absolute stillness showing the preparations for the chariot race between Pelops and Oinomaos. Twelve metopes, six at the eastern and six at the western end of the building, represented the Labours of Herakles. The sculptures, though found in a very fragmentary state, have been reconstructed to give a good idea of the design and style. Grandeur of conception and depth of feeling, qualities which the ancient critics attributed to the great sculptors and painters of the period, are the outstanding characteristics of these magnificent sculptures. In the centre of the west pediment (figure 15) stands Apollo, magnificent in

15. **Pediment of the Temple of Zeus at Olympia.** 470–456 BC. Marble. Olympia Museum, Greece. Central part of the west pediment of the temple of Zeus, at Olympia, showing the figure of Apollo and groups of a Lapith and Centaur in combat.

16. **Fore-part of a horse.** 490–480 BC. Marble. h. 44½ in. (1.13 m.). Acropolis Museum, Athens. The figure was found in the debris of the Persian sack of the Acropolis.

scale, commanding in gesture, remote in expression, dominating a wild scene of fighting. On the east pediment the figures are still and frontal, their stillness conveying a powerful feeling of impending drama. No artists of any other period of Greek art would have attempted a scene so dramatically still as that of the east pediment; no artist for another hundred years would achieve so powerful a piece of illustration as did the creator of the west pediment.

The sculpture of the early 5th century is full of the same kind of contrasts as we see in the pediments of Olympia. On the one hand, artists are striving to perfect new ideals of human and divine beauty. The decorative prettiness of drapery styles, the smiling faces of the archaic period, have disappeared. The figures of Zeus, Hippodameia, Pelops and Sterope, standing in the east pediment, represent that severe ideal of the human figure at which the artists of the period were aiming, an ideal that still lacks the harmonious balance achieved in the later part of the century. On the other hand, sculptors pursue a restless enquiry into the actions and emotions of men. The tortured struggle of the Centaurs is expressed in their faces; old age is brilliantly captured in the face and figure of the seer on the east pediment.

One of the few large-scale Greek bronzes that has come down to us, the statue of Zeus from the sea off Cape Artemision (plate 51) is the work of an unknown master sculptor, made between 470 and 460 BC. Zeus is in the act of hurling a thunderbolt, a pose in which the sculptor has tried to combine a monumental stillness and a momentary action. Myron's famous discus-thrower (figure 18), a work of about the same period, which is known only from copies, is a wonderful attempt to produce a perfect athletic action figure, an attempt that the later 5th-century sculptors were to renounce in favour of an ideal figure at rest. They were

17. **Head of Apollo.** Olympia Museum,
Greece. A detail of the head of Apollo,
in the centre of the west pediment at
Olympia.

to abandon, temporarily at least, the study of human emotions, and concentrate on achieving that limited perfection
of symmetry and proportion which is the essence of Greek
art. Pheidias, in his figures of gods and goddesses, raised
humanity to a new position of dignity; Polykleitos, with
devotion and supreme earnestness, created physical types
that best exemplify man's power to possess the world.

ATHENS UNDER PERICLES

It was the greatness of Athens in the time of Pericles, that
has given us the most vivid realisation of the Greek achievement. In the middle of the century, the Athenians, prompt-
ed by Pericles, decided to devote some of the surplus funds
accumulated in the treasury of the league of defence against
Persia to the rebuilding of the Acropolis at Athens (plate
49). They inaugurated a building programme which resulted in some of the finest buildings of the ancient world:
the Parthenon, chief temple of the patron goddess Athena,
the Propylaea, a monumental entrance to the sacred enclosure of the Acropolis, the Erechtheum (plate 50) and
other famous buildings. The programme included the erection of statues in bronze, marble and in the gold-and-ivory
technique that was used for the most splendid cult-statues
of the day. The great names in the sculpture of this period
are Pheidias, the friend of Pericles and, according to Plu-
tarch, the director of all his building projects, creator of the
gold and ivory cult images of Zeus at Olympia, and Athena
Parthenos at Athens, and the Argive Polykleitos, the per-
fector of the ideal athletic statue. Nothing survives of Pheidias' work, but he must have been concerned in the design
of the sculptures of the Parthenon, and it is quite likely that
he had a hand in some of the work. No original by Polykleitos has come down to us, but his great athletic figures
were much copied in later antiquity.

18. **The Lancellotti Discobolus.**
Roman period. Marble. h. 4 ft. 1 in.
(1.25 m.). Terme Museum, Rome.
A Roman copy of the famous bronze
figure of an athlete throwing a discus,
made by the Athenian sculptor, Myron,
about 450 BC.

19. **The Temple of Hephaestos, Athens.** 450–440 BC. This Doric temple stands on high ground near the Agora of Athens. Of all Greek temples, it is the best preserved.

20. **The Parthenon.** 447–432 BC. Marble. The temple of Athena Parthenos, on the Acropolis at Athens, was designed by two architects, Iktinos and Kallikrates. It housed the colossal gold and ivory image of Athena, patron goddess of the city.

21. **Dionysos.** 440–432 BC. Marble. h. 4 ft. 7 in. (1.40 m.). British Museum, London. The so-called 'Dionysos', a god or hero, is one of the surviving figures from the east pediment of the Parthenon at Athens.

22. **Two horsemen.** *c.* 440–432 BC. Marble. h. 3 ft. 3 in. (1 m.). British Museum, London. Two young horsemen riding in the Great Panathenaic procession in honour of Athena; part of the west frieze of the Parthenon.

The Parthenon (figure 20), built between 447 and 432 BC, was the most grandly conceived Doric temple of antiquity. Most of its sculptures are in the British Museum, brought to England by Lord Elgin in the early 19th century. Inside the temple stood Pheidias' gold and ivory image of Athena; on the building the groups of sculpture consisted of the two pedimental compositions, a complete series of sculptured metopes in the Doric frieze, and a continuous frieze round the upper part of the cella wall, an Ionic feature introduced into a number of Doric buildings during the period. The pedimental compositions represent, on the east, the birth of Athena, and, on the west, her contest with Poseidon to decide which of them should be the patron deity of Athens. The metopes show battles of Lapiths and Centaurs, gods and giants, Greeks and Amazons, Greeks and Trojans, all themes chosen to symbolise the triumph of Greek civilisation over barbarism, appropriate to a building which, in some sense, was thought of as a victory monument over the Persians. The frieze portrays the procession of the Great Panathenaia, held every four years by the people of Athens, the purpose of which was to present a new robe to a venerable image of Athena on the Acropolis. The procession began on the west side of the building, ran along the north and south in two separate streams, and converged on the ceremony of the robe that took place in the centre of the east front.

THE SCULPTURE OF THE PARTHENON

It is the business of great artists to reveal the ideals of an age, and in what has survived of the pedimental compositions the sculptural ideals of the 5th-century Greeks seem to stand fully revealed. The 'Dionysos' of the east pediment, one of the assembled company of gods to whom the birth of the goddess is announced, is one of the most grandly conceived nude figures in the whole history of art; he sits relaxed, pensive, a perfect blend of naturalism and ideal form, awe-inspiring in his grandeur. The river god ('Ilissos') from the west pediment (plate 52) raises himself on his left arm from a reclining position, a gentle movement that provides the artist with an opportunity to show the powerful forms of the body in a harmony of rest and tension. In the group of three goddesses from the other side of the same pediment, the majestic ideal of the female figure is embodied, with the massive forms of the body offset by a rich and subtle handling of the drapery. The stiffness, the flatness, the uncertainties of scale that one sees at Olympia, have now given place to a full three-dimensionality backed by superb technique. Comparatively few of the high relief metopes are well-preserved, and they, of all the sculptures from the Parthenon, are the least satisfying. Perhaps it is inherent in the nature of Greek art at this moment that they should be so; that the wild scenes of combat between Lapiths and Centaurs lack conviction, because perfection of form cannot be reconciled with violent action. It may be, as some people have thought, that less able sculptors worked on this particular part of the building. The same criticism is certainly not applicable to the low-relief of the frieze, which conveys the movement of the procession in a wholly convincing way—the bustle of the preparations, the gathering momentum of the horsemen, the handling of the sacrificial victims, the rush of the chariots, the quiet solemnity of the votive scene. Idealising it certainly is, but idealising in a way that seems to give a keener understanding of the reality of the events that lie behind it.

POLYKLEITOS AND ATHLETIC SCULPTURE

The Argive sculptor, Polykleitos, was held in antiquity to have achieved the Greek ideal of athletic beauty. We know his most famous work, the athlete carrying a lance, from many copies made in Roman times, when it was probably the most copied of Greek statues (figure 24). Polykleitos himself wrote a book explaining the principles of symmetry and proportion on which it was based. Since the abandonment of the *kouros* figure, the standing nude male figure had shifted its pose from one leg to the other, without achieving a position of perfect balance at rest. Some of the sculptors of the early 5th century had attempted to reconcile perfect pose and vigorous action, but Polykleitos goes back uncompromisingly to the position of rest. He chooses a pose with the left leg drawn back and touching the ground with the toes only—neither walking nor standing but partaking of both. The forms of the body are strongly knit and clearly differentiated, and a subtle opposition of tenseness and relaxation creates the perfect balance of the pose. Polykleitos, an intellectual among artists, was obsessed with rules of mathematical proportion in creating his figures, and was criticised in antiquity for a lack of versatility. His style is easily distinguishable, and copies of several of his famous

23. **Lapith and Centaur.** *c.* 440 BC. Marble. h. 4 ft. 8 in. (1.42 m.). British Museum, London. A metope from the south side of the Parthenon, showing a Lapith and a Centaur in combat.

works including the statue of a boy binding a fillet round his head and a figure of an Amazon, have been recognised.

A Roman copy of one of Pheidias' masterpieces may serve to conclude this brief account of sculpture in Greece down to the time of the Peloponnesian Wars. The head illustrated in figure 25 is a marble copy of the head of a bronze Athena by Pheidias, dedicated on the Acropolis of Athens about 440 BC by the Athenian colonists of Lemnos. The Roman writer, Lucian, chose the details of this head to grace his perfect woman, and indeed, it does seem to express to perfection the idea of Greek beauty, a beauty untouched by human emotion and existing nowhere in nature, yet raising the human face itself into a realm of superhuman reality.

THE DEVELOPMENT OF PAINTING

The 5th century was an age of great painters as of great sculptors, but of their work we know little. Polygnotus of Thasos, the most famous name in the period after the Persian wars, painted historical and mythological pictures at Athens and elsewhere, and ancient descriptions of some of them still survive. From what we hear of him he was a restlessly inventive genius, struggling, like the great innovators in sculpture, with problems of spatial representation, and a powerfully dramatic illustrator able to depict character as well as action in his work. We can only catch glimpses of the work of such masters in the surviving vase paintings of the time, but many of these are richly deserving of study in themselves. The best vases are superbly drawn, with their subjects taken from every branch of mythology, religion and everyday life.

In vase-painting, as in sculpture, the steps of the artistic revolution in the early 5th century can be followed fairly closely. The red-figure painters of the last two decades of the 6th century had delighted in showing the human figure in many different and complicated poses, but had not yet freed themselves from some of the awkwardness and inconsistency in archaic conventions. The best painters of the next generation, from 500–480 BC, have caught the spirit of a new age. By about 480 BC, the vase painters have achieved a consistent representation of figures at rest, or in movement, from a single viewpoint; the archaic face has made way for the 5th-century profile. On a *hydria*, now in Naples, the Kleophrades painter paints a scene showing the Sack of Troy, and with a fine command of gesture and expression, depicts the despair and horror of the victims. In plate 47, a scene taken from a vase in the British Museum, by the same painter, we see something of his powers as an illustrator. With wonderful economy of line, a clear understanding of anatomy in action, and a skilful use of foreshortening he gives a powerful rendering of his theme. The Berlin painter, a contemporary of the Kleophrades painter, stands for the severity of the early 5th-century idea of beauty; he likes to decorate his vases with single figures, slender, long-limbed and grandly conceived, striving for a formal perfection that can stand alone.

24. **The Doryphoros.** Roman period. Marble. h. 7 ft. (2.12 m.). National Museum, Naples. A Roman copy of the famous bronze statue of an athlete carrying a lance, made by Polykleitos of Argos about 440 BC.

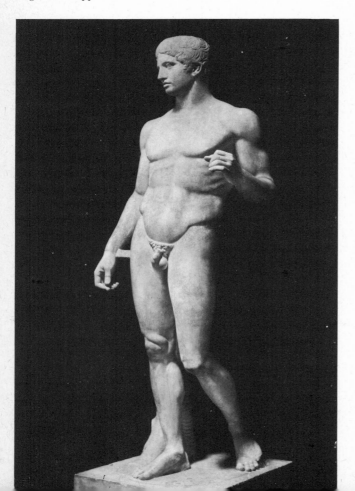

The Niobid painter, who was one of the chief vase painters in the generation between 480 and 460 BC, gives us, in his famous calyx crater in the Louvre, some idea of the methods used by the great masters of the early 5th century in their big compositions. The picture shows a scene apparently from the story of the Argonauts, a still scene like the composition of the east pediment at Olympia. The figures stand in easy poses, some skilfully shown in three-quarter view. The arrangement of the figures on different levels, with a very simple background of rocks as the only landscape detail, reflects the early attempts of the big-picture painters to suggest the third dimension. One figure is partly concealed by the rock behind which he is standing. The bigger white-ground vases of this period give us some idea of the palette and the technique of the panel painters. The technique is outline drawing filled in with washes of red, yellow and black in various tones, and still with no suggestion of attempts to shade or model the forms of the body in tones of colour. The grand manner of the master painters is captured by the Penthesilea painter in his scene on the inside of a cup, now in Munich (plate 48), which shows Achilles in the act of slaying Penthesilea. Although the composition, which may, in fact, be copied from one of the big pictures of the day, is ill-suited to the shape of the cup, the artist contrives to give a powerful impression of the pathos of the moment. It is instructive to compare Exekias' version of the same episode made some fifty years earlier (plate 37). From such pictures as these we get some idea of the style and technique of the great painters. Although their painting was still purely linear, they could, by their skill in conveying movement and expression, stimulate the imagination without recourse to the tricks of illusionist art.

The Pistoxenos painter, in his exquisite white-ground cup of Aphrodite riding on a goose, now in the British Museum, seems to have achieved the perfection of the classical Greek ideal; but the painter who tells us most about the lost masterpieces contemporary with the sculptures of Pheidias and Polykleitos is the Achilles painter. A pupil of the Berlin painter, he devotes his skill to the creation of single figures which have all the beauty of formal perfection for which the great artists strove. He is famous for his paintings on white-ground *lekythoi*, a type of vase made in the latter half of the 5th century to be placed in tombs. The quiet scenes, corresponding with those seen on the grave reliefs of the period, suited the simplicity of his style (plate 53).

ARCHITECTURE IN THE CITY-STATES

In architecture, as in other branches of the arts, the period down to the Peloponnesian Wars is one of the greatest achievement. After the Persian Wars, the city-states made great advances in civic and religious building but it is well to remember that there was still a great contrast between the splendours of their religious buildings and their civic architecture. Town planning and attention to the amenities of life were rudimentary. No stone theatre had yet been built; the Athenians of the 5th century watched the plays of Aeschylus, Sophocles and Euripides from wooden benches arranged on the south slope of the Acropolis, and, when they were over, they returned along narrow winding streets to homes built of humble materials and with no great pretensions to comfort. The buildings they used in their capacity as officials of the state were grander, and there were already public meeting places with shady colonnades.

THE ACROPOLIS OF ATHENS

The wealth of the city-states was lavished not on improving the private amenities of the citizens, but on beautifying the sanctuaries of the gods. The progress of temple building in the 5th century culminated in Pericles' great scheme for the rebuilding of the Acropolis. No other city-state commanded both the resources of Athens and the artists and architects capable of executing so grand a plan. One approaches the Acropolis rock from its western end, and enters the sacred enclosure through the Propylaea, a monumental gateway built by the architect Mnesikles between 437 and 432 BC (figure 26). The main architecture of the porches on either side of the gateway is massive Doric, but combined, in the outer porch, with Ionic columns. The gateway and its porches are flanked on the north and south by projecting halls, one of which, the southern, was never completed. The whole design of this complex building was brilliantly adapted to the difficult nature of the ground.

When you pass through the inner porch of the Propylaea, you get your first view of the Parthenon, which stands on the highest part of the rock. It is the greatest of the Doric temples and the ultimate achievement of the Doric style. The development of the Doric order can be followed through the early 5th century in the buildings of the Greek colonies and the mainland. The little temple of Hephaestos by the Agora at Athens (figure 19), the most perfectly preserved of Doric temples, had been built in the forties, and

26. **The Propylaea.** 437–432 BC. The Propylaea, the monumental entrance to the Acropolis, was erected under the administration of Pericles. The architect was Mnesikles.

27. **Demeter, Persephone and Triptolemos.** *c.* 440 BC. Marble. h. 7 ft. 11 in. (2.40 m.). National Museum, Athens. A votive relief found at Eleusis, in 1859, showing Demeter giving the ears of corn to her son, Triptolemos, while Persephone, her daughter, places a wreath on his head.

almost achieves the perfection, though it lacks the grandeur, of the Parthenon. Of the Parthenon itself, there is almost nothing left to be said; the subtle curvatures and refinements, introduced by the architects Iktinos and Kallikrates, give so solid and massive a structure a lightness and life which would seem to be denied to the Doric style by its very nature.

The Parthenon is the ultimate achievement of the Doric order, from which no further progress seems possible. From this time onwards we shall see architects experimenting with different orders and combinations. The Ionic order, which had been mainly confined to the cities of Ionian Greece, was becoming increasingly popular in the Greek cities of the mainland. It is used for two famous buildings on the Acropolis rock, the little temple of the Wingless Victory that stands isolated on a bastion to your right as you go up to the Propylaea, and the temple of Poseidon-Erechtheus, the Erechtheum, across from the Parthenon. The temple of Victory was apparently planned before the Parthenon, but the work was not begun until after 432; the Erechtheum was built between 421 and 409 BC. The plan of the Erechtheum is complicated, but basically consists of a rectangular temple building with porches at different levels on three sides; its architectural detail is exquisitely pretty and superbly carved. The entablature of the south porch is supported by six figures of maidens (plate 50), admirably suited by their classical severity to the role they perform. The Ionic order was, to some extent, still experimental; it did not achieve its canonical form until the next century. The Corinthian has not yet appeared at all in external architecture.

THE ACHIEVEMENTS OF THE FIFTH CENTURY

It is perhaps foolish even to attempt a summary assessment of the achievement of the Greeks in the arts up to the time of the Peloponnesian War. It is the period to which all antiquity, and we today, look back as the one of greatest achievement. Yet we should not be blinded to the limitations of the achievement. The restless enquiry of Greek artistic spirits in the late 6th century, and early 5th century, was, to some extent, halted in the achievement of its 'classical moment' in the second half of the 5th century. The architecture and sculpture of Periclean Athens seem to be the perfect expression of the aims and ideals of Greek culture, and it is a temptation to look on anything that follows it as a decline. But the history of European art would have been far different had progress been halted at this point. Painters had made only limited progress in the problems of their art, sculptors had achieved a limited ideal without a complete mastery of three-dimensional form, architects had brought a few traditional types of building to perfection, but had hardly begun to apply their art to wider uses.

THE PELOPONNESIAN WAR

When the Peloponnesian War began in 431 BC, the Parthenon had just been completed. The war dragged on until

28. Victory undoing her sandal.
c. 410 BC. Marble. h. 3 ft. 6 in. (1.06 m.).
Acropolis Museum, Athens. Relief from
the balustrade of the Temple of Athena
Nike, on the Acropolis at Athens.

29. Stele of Hegeso. *c.* 400 BC. Marble.
h. 4 ft. 11 in. (1.49 m.). National Museum,
Athens. Grave relief of a young woman,
Hegeso, daughter of Proxenos. Hegeso is
shown seated. Her maid hands her a jewel box.

404 BC, ending in ultimate victory for Sparta and her allies.
The Greek city-states would never again be able to tackle
artistic projects of such grandeur as the Periclean scheme
for the Acropolis. The state, it is true, continued to be the
chief patron of the arts, but the whole artistic atmosphere
began to change. Artists, who had devoted their lives to the
small communities in which they lived, now found it necessary to work abroad, for foreign rulers or for private citizens. The great sculptors and painters of the 4th century
emerge as individuals no longer devoted to the ideals of the
state and of the state religion, but free to experiment, even
to create, for themselves. They now saw much more of the
possibilities of subjects that had not been considered worthy
of study in the 5th century, and began to renew their enquiry into the problems of representational art.

There is a period in the art of the Greek city-states which
we may call the 'aftermath of the classical'; it covers the
years of the Peloponnesian War and the early years of the
4th century. In Athens the style of the Parthenon, reduced
to human proportions, continued to prevail, shorn of its
grandeur, and sometimes lapsing into a kind of decorative
prettiness and mannerism seen in some of the sculptures,
especially the relief sculptures, of the time. The charming
figures of Victories on the parapet put round the bastion
of the temple of Wingless Victory about 415 BC (plate 56),

show the exquisite skill of the sculptors in handling the
conventions of classical drapery—the clinging *chiton*, the
sweeping folds—in a purely decorative context. This
elegant late 5th-century style of relief sculpture was much
copied in later antiquity.

ATHENIAN GRAVE-RELIEFS

The Athenian grave-reliefs of the later 5th century represent the dead with the same ideal detachment that is used
to portray the people of Athens on the Parthenon frieze.
The *Stele of Hegeso* made about 420 BC (figure 29), which is
perhaps the most famous of the long series of Athenian
funerary monuments, has that atmosphere of quiet resignation which is common to them all. The dead girl is seated
on a chair, holding a necklace which her maidservant has
handed to her; there is no attempt at a portrait which
would break the harmony of this almost overpowering
scene of resignation in death. The grave-relief of Dexileos,
which commemorates a young man who fell at Corinth in
394 BC (figure 30), shows the cavalryman, in the heat of
battle, riding down an enemy.

THE SCULPTURE OF THE FOURTH CENTURY

It was inevitable that the grand manner, whose fundamental inspiration was the Olympian religion and the greatness

30. **Stele of Dexileos.** *c.* 394 BC. Marble.
h. 5 ft. 8 in. (1.72 m.). Kerameikos
Museum, Athens. Dexileos, who is shown
here riding down an enemy, fell at
Corinth in 394 BC, aged 20.

31. **Dancing Maenad.** Roman period.
Marble. h. 18 in. (45 cm.). Skulpturen-
sammlung, Dresden. This figure of a
maenad dancing in ecstasy may be a copy
of a famous work by the Greek sculptor,
Scopas of Paros of the 4th century BC.

of Athens, should not survive the Peloponnesian War. The
gods began to lose their mystery and frightening power.
The famous statue called the *Venus Genetrix*, which is probably copied from a famous sculpture of the last decades of
the 5th century, perhaps by a pupil of Pheidias, already
gives us a much more human conception of divinity. She
represents, too, a new interest in the beauty of woman,
paving the way for the studies of the female nude, a subject
that was to be the concern of Praxiteles and his contempo-
raries in the 4th century. Around 375 BC, Kephisodotos of
Athens, father of Praxiteles, made a statue, *Peace holding the
infant Wealth*, one of the earliest of such allegorical compositions in the history of art. His figure of Peace is conceived in
severe drapery, like the figures of Pheidias, but there is a
new gentleness and softness in the head inclining to gaze at
the little child she holds in her arms.

The great figures of the new generation of 4th-century
sculptors are Scopas, Praxiteles, Timotheus and Bryaxis.
We know something about the work of these sculptors from
direct Greek sources, as well as from Roman copies of their
work. Timotheus was concerned in the decoration of
the Temple of Asclepius at Epidaurus, and some fragments
of the architectural sculpture still survive. Scopas is said
to have been the architect of the Temple of Athena Alea
at Tegea, and may be supposed to have worked on its

sculpture as well. We know Praxiteles from Roman
copies of many of his sculptures. One statue, the *Hermes of
Olympia*, is believed by many to be an original from his
hand. Bryaxis is a less clearly defined personality, but
copies of some of his famous works survive. All four of these
men were said, according to one ancient tradition, to
have worked together in the decoration of the tomb of
Mausolus of Caria, the celebrated Mausoleum, in the
middle of the 4th century BC, and attempts have been made
to recognise their work in the sculptures that have survived
from the building.

SCOPAS AND PRAXITELES

Scopas was clearly an artist of genius. He was famous for
his attempts to express strongly emotional themes. He made
a group depicting Love, Yearning and Desire, at Megara,
and his figure of a maenad dancing in ecstasy was one of
his most admired pieces. The art of the second half of the
5th century had, as we have seen, halted the Greek urge to
portray violent feelings and emotions; the 4th-century
sculptors revived and developed it. The head illustrated in
plate 60 comes from one of the scenes decorating the pediments of the temple designed by Scopas at Tegea; the
heavy features and deep-set haunted eyes are something
new in the history of Greek art, and should probably be

32. **Head of Hermes.** *c.* 340 BC. Marble. h. (of statue) 7 ft. (2.13 m.). Olympia Museum, Greece. Head of the statue of Hermes carrying the child Dionysos found in the Temple of Hera at Olympia in 1877. It is probably the work of the sculptor Praxiteles.

attributed to the influence of Scopas. There is a tradition that Scopas was the sculptor of one of the column-bases in the new temple of Artemis at Ephesus, rebuilt after a fire in 356. The best preserved of these bases has a solid Polykleitan figure of Hermes, seen standing and looking upwards between the figures of two goddesses. It has been attributed to Scopas, and perhaps there is something of his style in the yearning face and deep-set eyes (plate 61).

Scopas is a world apart from Pheidias and Polykleitos, and so is his contemporary Praxiteles who worked both in bronze and marble, but seems to have preferred the latter. The painter Nikias used to colour his statues. No statue illustrates better the contrast between his work and the art of the 5th century, than that of *Hermes carrying the infant Dionysos*, which was found in the Temple of Hera at Olympia in 1877, and is probably an original by his hand. The god, in a leaning pose, rests his left elbow in the trunk of a tree and holds the child in the crook of his arm. In his missing right hand he held a bunch of grapes, or some other object, for the child to play with. The figure represents a completely new ideal of male beauty, 'the climax', Sir Kenneth Clark calls it, 'of passion for physical beauty'. The forms of the body are softer and slimmer, the transitions less sharply defined, firm, but without athletic strength. The perfection of the finish gives to the surface the texture

of real flesh, just as the drapery, to the casual glance, looks like real drapery.

The temperament of Praxiteles was delicate, refined and graceful, and found its best expression in studies of beautiful women. The female nude had not been a subject for 5th-century art, though the way in which post-Pheidian sculptors force the flimsy drapery to reveal the forms of the nude seems to herald its appearance. From the time of Praxiteles the female nude becomes a chief subject for art. We illustrate (figure 33) a Roman copy of one of the famous Aphrodites of the time, the so-called *Capitoline Venus*, now in the Capitoline Museum, Rome. Praxiteles' most famous statue was his nude *Aphrodite in Cnidos*, for which he is said to have used his mistress, Phryne, as a model. The tradition is revealing; the classical vision of a glorious but impossible humanity has now given place to an ideal much closer to actuality, and Praxiteles was certainly one of the chief innovators who led Greek art in this new direction.

PORTRAITURE IN THE FOURTH CENTURY

A closer study of the individual, and the rapid development of the art of portraiture, is a characteristic of the art of the 4th century. In the early 5th century there had already been some notable attempts at individual portraiture; we have copies of 5th-century generals, including those of

33. **The Capitoline Venus.** Roman period. Marble. h. 6 ft. 4 in. (1.93 m.). Capitoline Museum, Rome. A Roman copy of a Greek original made about the middle of the 4th century BC; found in Rome between 1667 and 1670.

Themistocles and Pericles, which are convincing attempts at characterisation made with a careful study of the features of the individual. But the search for ideal form, with its implied perfection of mind and spirit, led artists away from attempts at true realistic portraiture. In the 4th century, on the other hand, the individual bulks much larger in the Greek scheme of things, and careful observation of distinctive features forms the basis of the characterisation. The statue (plate 65), usually identified as Mausolus himself, from the ruins of the Mausoleum at Halicarnassus, is a fine study of a man of obvious strength of character, made by a Greek sculptor about 350 BC. The bronze *Head of a Berber*, from Cyrene, in the British Museum (plate 69), which may belong to this period, combines a detailed study of nature with almost classical regularity of features. The artists of the 4th century extended their studies to all ages and types of man. In the famous grave-relief from the Ilissos, made about 340 BC, the weeping child at the dead man's feet is portrayed with loving care, and in the old man we have a fine study of old age (figure 34).

LYSIPPUS OF SICYON

So far in this chapter we have not mentioned Lysippus. This famous and prolific sculptor, the last great name in the history of Greek sculpture, seems in fact to have had a remarkably long career, the last part of which was spent as court sculptor to Alexander the Great. The best creative part of his career probably fell in his later years. Perhaps he should be looked upon as a slightly younger contemporary of Scopas and Praxiteles. We know his work only from copies, though, curiously enough, a group of figures, found at Delphi, seem to be contemporary copies in marble of a bronze group he made at Pharsalus in northern Greece. The best-preserved of these figures is the statue of Agias, a boxer. His most famous figure, *The Apoxyomenos*, an athlete scraping himself with a strigil (figure 35), is known from Roman copies. He also made the portrait of Alexander the Great, from which the *Azara Herm* (figure 36) is taken.

One important aspect of Lysippus' work as a sculptor seems to have been his attempt to introduce a new canon of proportions for the male figure. Scopas and Praxiteles had been content with adapting the Polykleitan proportions to the new types of figure they chose; Lysippus favours a taller and slimmer figure with a smaller head. In the *Apoxyomenos*, he also goes a good deal further than the masters of the 5th century towards achieving a figure that can be looked at with equal satisfaction from all angles; the arms of his athlete stretch out towards the spectator, and even in the inferior Roman copy there is a fine sense of imminent movement. Lysippus, the last great athletic sculptor of antiquity, restored firmness to the forms of the body, but introduced a lightness and movement, and a three-dimensionality, that were to serve as powerful new influences on the art of the Hellenistic world. A fine original, contemporary with the later work of Lysippus, is the Antikythera bronze youth, a figure of an athlete holding a ball,

found in the sea off Antikythera in 1900. The figure, made perhaps about 340 BC, follows the Polykleitan canon of proportions (plate 62), but, like Lysippus, the sculptor has chosen a simple action of the arm to give life and movement to the static figure.

THE DEVELOPMENT OF ILLUSIONISTIC PAINTING

There was a statement in one of the elder Pliny's Greek sources that painting began about 420 BC. To Apollodorus, a painter of Athens in the last quarter of the 5th century, is given the credit for having 'opened the door of art' by first using shades of colour to model his figures, and so give them 'real substance'. The ancient critics, in other words, distinguished the art of painting from that of coloured drawing, which had prevailed down to that time. The period that followed Apollodorus was one of rapid advances in the solution of problems of modelling in colour, and the creation of pictorial space. These advances were the work of the great painters of the 4th century, of whose work we have scarcely an inkling. We cannot even follow the progress of the art of painting by means of first-class vase-paintings; at the end of the 5th century, vase-painting goes into decline and, in any case, the traditional red-figured technique can give us very little idea of what the big painters were achieving in the direction of illusionist art. Just occasionally there are

still echoes of the big pictures in the vases of Athens, and of the south Italian Greek cities, which also provide a vast mass of red-figured vases during the 4th century.

The vase illustrated in plate 55 is contemporary with the Peloponnesian Wars; the painter shows his principal figure in three-quarter view, and has gone as far as a draughtsman can go to give his picture depth and three-dimensionality without the aid of shading. This is just the time when Apollodorus was taking the first steps towards modelling his figures in colour, and in a few of the vases of the time a limited use of shading and a more skilful application of thin glaze washes in drapery folds, and other details, seem to reflect his work. The 'grisaille' painting on a marble slab, found at Herculaneum, which is generally believed to be a copy of a late 5th-century picture, makes use of a good deal of shading on drapery and skin (plate 54). The Meidias painter of the last quarter of the 5th century is a mannered and affected draughtsman, whose style corresponds with the charming decorative sculpture of the late 5th century. He makes much use of foreshortening, but has not advanced beyond the early 5th century in his method of showing depth by distributing figures over the vase surface at different levels (plate 57). There is no trace of linear perspective in his work, or in the work of his contemporary, the Pronomos painter, who uses the same scheme in one or two

35. The Apoxyomenos of Lysippus.
Roman period. Marble. h. 6 ft. 9 in.
(2.05 m.). Vatican Museums. A copy of
a bronze original by Lysippus of Sicyon,
showing an athlete scraping himself with
a strigil. Second half of the 4th century BC.

ambitious mythological pictures. These often show a rather more developed use of landscape, and seem to be modelled on contemporary wall paintings.

The first inkling of major advances in the problems of linear perspective is to be seen in some of the south Italian vases of the 4th century. The fragment, illustrated in plate 58, from a Tarentine vase of about 350 BC, shows an attempt to depict a building receding in depth. It is effective, without suggesting any clear understanding of the theory of perspective. Experiments in this kind of illusion are associated with the work of stage-designers in the theatre, and it seems to have been in stage painting that the Greeks of the Hellenistic period ultimately worked out the basic knowledge of consistent linear perspective. The fragment also shows that flat washes and outline drawing are giving place to modelling in colour, and there is a subtle use of colour tones in the rendering of the architecture.

THE ALEXANDER MOSAIC

Despite these few indications of rapid advances in the art of painting during the 4th century, it nevertheless comes as a great surprise to realise that the famous Alexander Mosaic found at Pompeii (plates 66, 68), is almost certainly a copy of a painting of the late 4th century. Here the artist, perhaps a certain Philoxenos of Eretria, working in a limited four-colour scheme, depicts the dramatic moment in the victory of Issus, when Alexander and Darius come face to face in battle. The bodies of men and animals are skilfully modelled in tones of colour; highlights and shadows play on the figures, and recession in depth is achieved by linear and a suggestion of aerial perspective. All these had been devices completely unknown to painters of the time of Pericles.

It has been suggested that several of the large figure compositions used in Pompeian wall decorations, are copies of well-known masterpieces of the period. These pictures are usually mythological scenes, in which the figures are arranged in the foreground against a setting of buildings or landscape. The setting, though secondary to the figures, is skilfully handled, using illusionistic techniques, and displays a fair understanding of linear and aerial perspective. The Hellenistic painted tombstones from Pagasai in Greece, though poorly preserved, show similar relations of figures to setting and similar attempts to create spatial depth, and it is likely that such pictures as the Perseus and Andromeda scene illustrated in plate 111, even though they cannot be taken as accurate copies of 4th-century pictures, give us some idea of how the painters of the period composed their pictures.

NEW FORMS IN ARCHITECTURE

The architecture of the late 5th and 4th centuries may seem to be anti-climax after the achievements of the 5th century. Yet the period is one of great importance in the history of architecture. The development of town-planning, and a greater variety of specifically designed civic buildings, are two features of the age. New towns, laid out to the regular

m. 0   100   200   300
f 0   200   400   600   800

G. Plan of the town of Priene.

plan associated with the name of Hippodamus of Miletus, would be equipped with a regularly planned market place surrounded by colonnades, and meeting places for the assembly and council. Much greater attention was now paid to the amenities of life; well paved streets with efficient drainage became a normal feature of Greek towns. The first stone theatres, which are such familiar monuments of the Greek scene, were built in this period; the theatre at Epidaurus (plate 64) which, even today, is still well preserved, was designed by a famous architect, Polykleitos the Younger, in the second half of the 4th century. Pausanias, who wrote his guide book to Greece in the 2nd century AD, calls it the most beautiful theatre of the ancient world. There was rapid development, too, in the handling of the classical orders of architecture. The greatest achievements of the Ionic order belong to this century. The temple of Artemis at Ephesus, destroyed by fire in 356, was rebuilt on an even grander scale in the years that followed, and was counted in later antiquity among the Seven Wonders of the World. Another of the Seven was the famous tomb of Mausolus at Halicarnassus, a building of outlandish design, with an Ionic colonnade surmounted by a stepped pyramid built by a Greek architect for the Carian dynasty. The Corinthian order began to be used for external architecture. The Corinthian capital had made its first tentative appearance in the interior of the temple of Apollo at Bassae, in the Peloponnese. Its popularity increased during the 4th century. A Corinthian 'order', combining the Corinthian column with an Ionic entablature, was used on the little round monument, put up in Athens in 334 BC by Lysicrates, the successful patron of a chorus in the theatre.

H. Reconstructed drawing of the Ionic Order.

36. Herm of Alexander the Great.
c. 330 BC. Marble. h. 2 ft. 3 in. (68 cm.). Louvre, Paris. Roman copy of the head of the famous portrait statue of Alexander with a lance by the sculptor Lysippus.

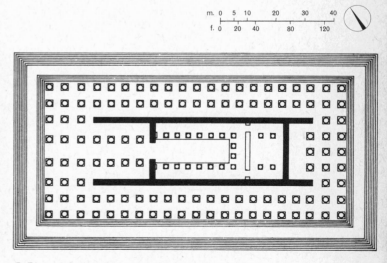

I. Plan of the later Temple of Artemis at Ephesus.

The Hellenistic World

Down to the time of Alexander the Great (356–323 BC), the small independent communities which we call city-states had been the basis of Greek life. With Alexander's conquests, the Greek world was transformed and its area vastly expanded. The new kingdoms founded by Alexander's successors, and not the old city-states, now dictated the course of Greek history. The period from Alexander down to 31 BC, when the last of the successor-kingdoms, that of the Ptolemies in Egypt, was absorbed by Rome, is called Hellenistic to describe the process by which a large part of the previously non-Greek world was 'Hellenised'. Greek influence now reached as far east as India; 'Hellenised' kingdoms were set up in the eastern possessions of the Persian Empire. In Egypt the Ptolemies rule over Greeks and Egyptians; the Seleucids of Syria controlled a kingdom that included peoples of many different racial stocks. The extent to which Greek mixed with non-Greek varied from place to place, and Alexander's ideal of brotherhood between Greeks and Orientals was never fully realised. But everywhere there was a mingling of Greek and oriental ideas, which served as the basis for the unified rule later imposed on the Hellenistic world by the Romans.

COMPLEX CHARACTER OF HELLENISTIC ART

The art of the Hellenistic world is difficult to understand; it lacks the clear simple lines that dictate the development of the Greek tradition. We can only understand it, if we grasp the fact that the whole conception of art now changes. I think it is true to say that the Greeks, for all they had achieved, had not yet discovered the pleasure of art; the Greeks of the Hellenistic period gave us a new conception of art as something to please and amuse, not simply to educate and instruct. We must abandon the idea of the Greek artist as the respected craftsman working for a small community, the servant of its ideals and way of life. Artists now moved freely about the Greek world; they worked as court-artists for the new rulers, for city-communities, and for private individuals. They were honoured for their talents, their products admired as 'works of art'. They were called upon to exercise their talents on a much wider range of subjects, for the Hellenistic age is characterised by a spirit of restless enquiry into every branch of art and science. The development of the exact sciences inspires the desire to portray things as they are, encourages the representation of men and nature in all their aspects. The desire produces the means for achieving the illusion of reality in sculpture and painting; the most admired works are those which are nearest to complete illusion. The ideals of the art of the city-states seem very remote from all this.

In the sense that it introduces a vast new range of themes into art, the Hellenistic period is greatly creative, and has left us some of the most admired works of ancient sculpture and painting; in the sense that it makes use of established types, copies or adapts them to new purposes, it lacks the highest kind of artistic creativity. The restless search for variety and new techniques among contemporary artists inevitably produced this harking back to the directness and simplicity of earlier ideals. Hellenistic rulers and wealthy private individuals wanted copies of old masters; the kings of Pergamon sent artists to Greece to copy famous pictures, and a copy in marble of the *Athena Parthenos* has been found in their capital. When art, as it so often did, served purely decorative purposes, and was backed by a supreme mastery of technique, it was bound to lack the certainty of taste that characterised the work of the classical masters. Hellenistic art can be all things — bombastic and rhetorical, pretty and decorative, vulgar or restrained — and in the end one tires of its variety and virtuosity.

OUR KNOWLEDGE OF HELLENISTIC ART

There is an embarrassing mass of surviving sculpture, both originals and copies, from the Hellenistic period, and almost no original painting. The sculpture is very difficult to classify into regions and styles, and we shall make very little attempt to do so here. It is easy to over-emphasise the importance of particular centres, and to attribute a particular 'style' to them on very little evidence; Alexandria, for example, has been associated with the development of the Praxitelean style towards greater softness, but whether this tendency is purely Alexandrian we cannot say. We know the art of Pergamon in the 2nd century BC comparatively well, but the 'schools' of other important centres are hardly known at all. In a period of art which is characterised by its variety of aims, it is dangerous to apply modern artistic labels, such as 'baroque' and 'rococo', especially if these are given any close chronological or regional significance in the period. Ease of communication throughout the Hellenistic world produces, in many different places, works of similar style: the 'baroque' and the 'rococo' can exist side by side. Only in architecture, where local conditions produce their own solutions to problems of building, can we recognise regional styles clearly, and here, too, new fashions spread quickly to other areas.

HELLENISTIC ART AND THE ROMANS

Before concluding this introduction, there is one further problem to be mentioned. Hellenistic art is not sharply divided from Roman art; in many aspects the two merge with one another. In the final chapter of this book an attempt is made to explain the various influences that give rise to the development of a specifically Roman tradition in art and architecture. Here we must stress that the Romans have a large part to play in the later development of Hellenistic art itself. From the 2nd century onwards, the Romans were increasingly involved in the affairs of the Hellenistic kingdoms which, one by one, succumbed to their power. The Roman attitude to art was very similar to that of the Hellenistic kings and wealthy citizens, whom they began to displace as its chief patrons. Like the kings of Pergamon, they needed artists to carve commemorative monuments and paint triumphal pictures, they admired the decorative qualities of contemporary art, and used it to

38. **The Venus de Milo.** *c.* 100 BC.
Marble. h. 6 ft. 8 in. (2.03 m.). The
Louvre, Paris. This famous statue of
the goddess Aphrodite was found on the
island of Melos in 1820.

37. **Homer.** Roman period. Marble.
h. 20½ in. (52 cm.). British Museum,
London. This herm is a Roman copy of
an ideal portrait of the Hellenistic period,
showing the poet as a blind old man.

decorate their houses and public buildings. Like the Pergamene kings, they also admired the work of the 5th- and 4th-century artists, collected their masterpieces and encouraged the rapid development of copying and adaptation, both in painting and sculpture. There is a word, Greco-Roman, which has rather gone out of fashion, but it serves well to describe the latest phase of Hellenistic art, especially the 1st century BC, because it clearly implies this intimate relationship between Greek art and Roman patronage, in the century before the foundation of the Roman Empire by Augustus.

HELLENISTIC FIGURE-SCULPTURE

The career of Lysippus of Sicyon extended from the earlier part of the 4th century down to the time of Alexander of Macedon, whose court sculptor he was. He is, therefore, the first of the Hellenistic sculptors: he is also the last of the great names, and this, in itself, is a very significant fact. The artists of the early Hellenistic period carry on the traditions of the masters of the 4th century without winning great reputations for themselves. It was a pupil of Lysippus who, in the 3rd century, made for the city of Rhodes the bronze colossus of the sun god, which was counted among the Seven Wonders of the World. His own name, however, is not among the truly famous. The followers of Praxiteles could add little to the master's ideal of the female nude, because, in truth, there was nothing to add; the blend between ideal form and reality was perfect. The famous statue, the *Venus de Milo*, in the Louvre, is a work of about 100 BC (figure 38); the style is still essentially that of Praxiteles, only the more complicated pose of the body, which lacks the simplicity of the Praxitelean ideal, distinguishes it from the work of the master, and makes it typical of the age to which it belongs. Hellenistic sculptors did try to get away from the traditional poses, to develop the momentary stance that was brought in by Lysippus, and to render convincing action figures, but the result tends to be unnatural and exaggerated, even theatrical. There is a very delicate balance between a figure that seems about to move and one that is artificially frozen into immobility, and only the greatest artists can achieve the one and avoid the other.

In the later Hellenistic period, there seems to have been some attempt to create ideal figures based on the best available human models, instead of an ideal conception of the human form. The models do not often appeal. A leaning Herakles of Lysippus, translated into a heavy muscular, even muscle-bound athlete, achieved some popularity. The well-known bronze, called *The Hellenistic Ruler*, in the Terme Museum, Rome, has a heaviness and lack of proportion in which one recognises a human model. The attempt at realism in the rendering of the nude was short-lived, and when it was abandoned, artists resorted instead to a kind of eclecticism, which sometimes takes details and forms from a number of different statues, and sometimes adapts traditional figures by altering the forms of the head and

39. **The Hellenistic Ruler.** 2nd century
BC. Bronze. h. 7 ft. 9 in. (2.36 m.). Terme
Museum, Rome. This well-known bronze
has a heaviness and lack of proportion in
which one recognises a human model.

body. A small bronze figure of Marsyas in the British Museum is a typical Hellenistic adaptation, based on the figure in a group of Athena and Marsyas by the 5th-century sculptor, Myron. The artist has completely transformed the head to suit modern taste, has given the figure a more strongly modelled muscular form, and preserves only the pose of Myron's original masterpiece. The eclectic tendencies in late Hellenistic figure-sculpture culminate in the work of Pasiteles, a south Italian Greek from Naples, who worked mainly for rich Roman patrons in the early 1st century BC, and founded a school that copied and adapted classical masterpieces. A Pasitelean figure may combine the styles of a number of different periods of Greek art—a body in the severe style, a head of the 4th century, a Polykleitan pose. Such work implies the same deep knowledge of the development of Greek art that we find in contemporary art-critics and historians of art, a little of whose work is preserved to us in the pages of Roman writers.

It is only very rarely that Hellenistic art achieves greatness in single-figure sculpture, but none can deny this quality to the figure of Victory, from the island of Samothrace, which was made about 200 BC to commemorate a naval victory (figure 40). The goddess is represented alighting on the prow of a vessel. The pose of the figure is superb, but perhaps the most remarkable quality of the piece is the brilliant synthesis of movement and drapery, something which had never been done quite so well before. In an age when most sculptors had abandoned earlier attempts to use the drapery of the female figure as a powerful means of expression, and had resorted to technical tricks to show their virtuosity, this work stands out as an immense achievement.

HELLENISTIC SCULPTURED GROUPS

A very important development in the art of sculpture during Hellenistic times lies in the handling of figure-groups in the round. As we have seen, free figure sculpture achieved something approaching full three-dimensionality in the work of Lysippus, and this new knowledge was applied in the succeeding period to complicated groups of a kind that had previously been attempted only in relief sculpture. The technical problems involved in the design and execution of such groups were now well within the scope of the artists, and their work has produced some remarkable examples of artistic virtuosity. These groups illustrate the vast range of Hellenistic sculpture; they range from the noble 'baroque' conceptions of the Pergamene Gaulish groups to playful combinations of satyrs and maenads. Among the best known groups in the grand manner are those deriving from the monuments put up by the Attalid kings of Pergamon in Athens and Pergamon, to commemorate the victories over the Gaulish invaders in the 3rd century BC. The famous group of a Gaulish chieftain who has slain his wife and is on the point of plunging his sword into his own breast, is a magnificent piece of theatre (figure 41); for all its exaggeration, it makes a powerful appeal to the emo-

40. The Victory of Samothrace.
Early 2nd century BC. Marble. h. 8 ft.
(2.45 m.). Louvre, Paris. Statue of
victory alighting on the prow of a ship.
Found on the island of Samothrace in
1863, it was originally made to commemorate a naval victory.

41. Gaulish chieftain and his wife.
Marble. h. 50 in. (1.8 m.). Terme
Museum, Rome. The Gaul has killed
his wife and is about to kill himself.
A Roman copy of a group set up in the
late 3rd century BC, to commemorate the
Gaulish victories of the Pergamene kings.

tions. So, indeed, does the even more famous group *Laocoon and his two Sons* (figure 42). Pliny the Elder thought that this group, the work of Rhodian sculptors, was the finest sculpture of antiquity and many, since Renaissance times, have held the same view; we today do not give it quite the same unqualified praise, but we can admire its strong emotional power expressed through the bodies and the faces, and the brilliance of its composition and technique. There is much to admire, too, in the more frivolous groups of figures in which Hellenistic artists and their patrons so obviously delighted. A typical example is the group, *Aphrodite, Pan and Eros*, now in the National Museum at Athens (plate 74). The goddess Aphrodite is warding off Pan with her slipper, while Eros, his tormentor, is also in attendance. The group, which was made, perhaps about 100 BC for a rich merchant on the island of Delos, typifies the lighter, playful side of Hellenistic art, which delights in humanised gods and monsters, and allegories of the ordinary human emotions.

REALISM AND PORTRAITURE

We have already stressed the range of human themes that becomes the subject-matter for Hellenistic art, and the restless enquiry and pitiless realism with which they are portrayed. The sculptors now model with convincing skill the

plump bodies of children, the withered flesh of old women, and their skill and virtuosity were greatly admired. In one of Herondas' mimes, there is a quotation about a well-known group of a child strangling a goose: 'If the marble were not before your eyes', says the poet, 'you would swear he was about to speak'. In the search for variety, sculptors did not shrink from the portrayal of physiological and pathological defects, such as we see in the little Hellenistic ivory figure of a hunchback, illustrated in figure 43.

The desire to see and represent things as they are in reality is shown best in the developments that took place in the art of portraiture during the Hellenistic period. Portrait sculptors of the 5th century BC had indeed paid some attention to an individual's features; one feels it is probable that we would recognise Pericles from the portrait of him by Kresilas, which exists in marble copies, but the head is simplified in detail and obviously idealised. In the 4th century the same idealising tendencies survive in the portrait-statue of Sophocles, one of a series of retrospective statues of 5th-century dramatists set up in Athens between 340 and 330 BC (figure 44). But the urge towards realism is clear enough. The portraits of contemporary 4th-century celebrities attempt to get close to the character of the man through a careful study of his features. The copies of portraits of Alexander the Great, which seem to go back to originals by Lysippus, his court sculptor, are 'idealised', but their idealism is achieved within the frame of a realistic likeness, by expression and set of the head, and not by simplification of the individual's face.

The ancient judgement on the portraits by Lysistratus, Lysippus' brother, stresses this essential difference from earlier work by saying that he made them lifelike, whereas previous artists had striven to make them as beautiful as possible. But no court portraiture can be too frank, and portraits of Hellenistic rulers are never realistic. Ideal physical form still implied the perfection of mind and spirit, and portrait figures continued to be ideal types, often based upon traditional figures, even when the faces try to express the personality of the men with a remarkable vividness. The coin portrait of Antimachus (plate 76), the marble head of Euthydemus, both kings of the remarkable dynasty that ruled the Greco-Bactrian kingdom, and the fine portraits of Ptolemy I (figure 45) and his successors in Egypt, show what the best portrait sculptors of the Hellenistic courts could achieve. In the last centuries BC, the traditions of Hellenistic court-portraiture served the new masters of

the Greek world, the Romans; an interesting series of late Hellenistic portraits (see plate 77) mainly of wealthy businessmen living on the commercial island of Delos, are the work of Greek portraitists for rich private individuals, many of them Romans, whose own traditions demanded the same kind of realistic portraiture, which did not ignore the irregularities and blemishes of the individual face, and could convey a powerful impression of the character of the man.

RELIEF-SCULPTURE

The art of relief-sculpture made great advances in the Hellenistic period. The tendency towards realism, and the invention of new illusionistic techniques in other branches of the arts, shows its influence in the treatment of reliefs. The scene from the Amazon frieze of the Mausoleum at Halicarnassus (plate 63) makes clear the principles of earlier relief-sculpture. Groups of figures are arranged against a plain background in simple, balanced compositions, there is very little overlapping of figures and hardly any attempt to suggest space. The syntax is simple and disciplined; the idea of the struggle is conveyed entirely by means of power-

(Continued on page 97)

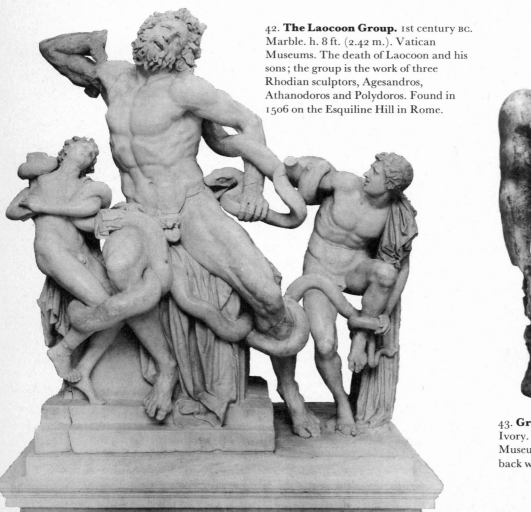

42. **The Laocoon Group.** 1st century BC. Marble. h. 8 ft. (2.42 m.). Vatican Museums. The death of Laocoon and his sons; the group is the work of three Rhodian sculptors, Agesandros, Athanodoros and Polydoros. Found in 1506 on the Esquiline Hill in Rome.

43. **Grotesque figure.** Late Hellenistic. Ivory. h. 4⅛ in. (10.5 cm.). British Museum, London. Statuette of a hunchback with the symptoms of Pott's disease.

45. (above). **Relief from the Palace
at Persepolis.** 1 ft. 8 in. (50 cm.).
British Museum, London. This fragment
of a processional frieze comes from the
eastern façade of the palace built by
Darius I. It shows a group of Royal guards
in procession. The kings of Persia employed many Greek artists from the cities
of Ionia and the mainland, and their
influence can be clearly seen in the treatment of the drapery on these figures,
though the spirit of the frieze is completely
un-Greek.

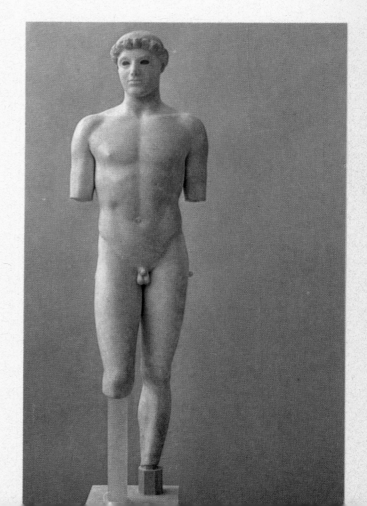

46. (right). **The Kritian Boy.** *c.* 480 BC.
Marble. h. 2 ft. 9 in. (84 cm.). Acropolis
Museum, Athens. This statue of a youth
was found on the Acropolis at Athens, and
is believed to be one of the sculptures cast
down by the Persians in 480 BC. It was
probably carved shortly before that date.
The figure has departed from the strict
canon of the 6th century *kouroi*, and looks
forward towards the balance, rhythm
and mastery of structure that characterise
the art of the 5th century. It is called the
Kritian boy, because its style is similar to
the figure of Harmodius in the famous
group of the tyrant slayers by the sculptors
Kritios and Nesiotes, which is known to
us from Roman copies.

47. (left). **The Kleophrades Painter. Theseus killing the Minotaur.** *c.* 470 BC. Vase painting. h. (of vase) 12½ in. (32 cm.). British Museum, London. The hero has grasped the muzzle of the wounded Minotaur and is just about to slay him. The scene illustrates the skill of red-figure painters in giving a powerful rendering of action by means of pure line drawing with skilful use of foreshortening. The vase was found at Vulci.

48. (below). **The Penthesilea Painter. The death of Penthesilea.** *c.* 460 BC. Vase painting. diam. 18 in. (46 cm.). Antikensammlungen, Munich. The scene is painted on the inside of a red-figure cup. It is thought that the scene was copied from a large scale painting, perhaps one of the big panel pictures of the day. The fallen Amazon, whose body follows the curve of the cup, must be thought of as lying on the ground below the main figures. Considerable use is made of additional colours in the picture: blue, red, brown, yellow and some gilding. The scene is painted with a fine dramatic feeling.

49. (above). **The Acropolis of Athens, from the South-West.** The Acropolis, which had been the citadel of Mycenaean times, became the chief sanctuary of the city-state. The buildings that may be seen in this view are, on the left, the monumental entrance, the *Propylaea*, with the temple of Athena Nike on the bastion to the right of it, the Parthenon, chief temple of the patron goddess Athena, and the Erechtheum.

50. (left). **The Caryatid Porch of the Erechtheum.** 421–409 BC. Marble. The Erechtheum, temple of Athena Polias and Poseidon-Erechtheus, was begun in 421 BC, and completed some time after 409 BC. In the south porch of the temple the place of columns is taken by standing figures of maidens, called Caryatids; the second figure from the left in this picture is a portland cement cast of the one in the British Museum, which was removed from the building by Lord Elgin.

51. (right). **Statue of Zeus or Poseidon from Cape Artemision.** *c.* 460 BC. Bronze. 6 ft. 10 in. (2.09 m.). National Museum, Athens. This statue, found in the sea off Cape Artemision, has been interpreted either as Zeus hurling a thunderbolt or Poseidon hurling his trident. It is one of the very few original Greek bronzes that have come down to us and is the work of a master-sculptor of the period.

52. (below). **Reclining figure of a river-god.** *c.* 440 BC. Marble. l. 5 ft. 3½ in. (1.61 m.). British Museum, London. The subject of the west pediment of the Parthenon, to which this figure belongs, was the contest between Athena and Poseidon to decide which should be the patron deity of the city of Athens. The fine torso, probably representing the Athenian river Ilissos, comes from the left corner of the pediment. A watery existence seems to be suggested by the clinging drapery on the left arm of the figure.

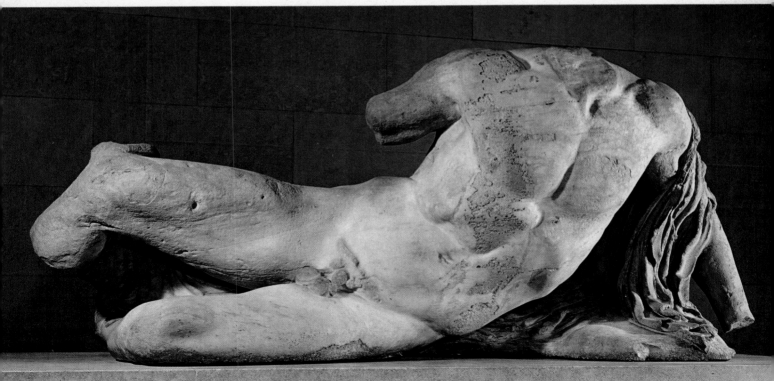

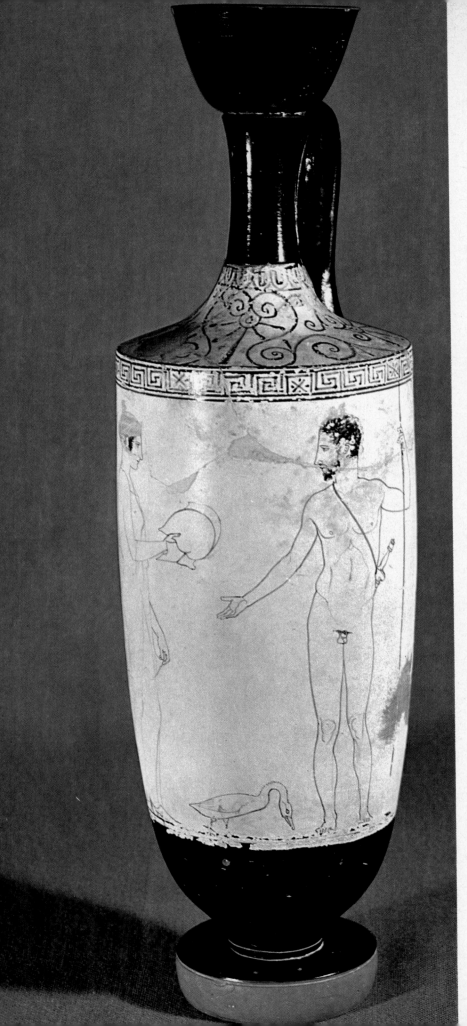

53. (left). **The Achilles Painter. White-ground lekythos.** *c.* 440 BC. Pottery. h. 15½ in. (39 cm.). British Museum, London. This type of vase was a common grave-offering in 5th-century Athens, and the painted subjects are often related to this funerary use. On this vase a woman is shown handing a soldier his helmet. The figures are painted in brown, black and red on a white slip, which covers the body of the vase.

55. (right). **The Peleus Painter. The Muse Terpsichore.** *c.* 440 BC. Pottery. h. (of vase) 23 in. (58 cm.). British Museum, London. This detail is from an Attic red-figure vase found at Vulci in Etruria. The figure seated in the centre is the muse Terpsichore; the youth in front of her is Mousaios, while behind her stands Melousa. The picture belongs to the time of the Parthenon. The use of the three-quarter view for the principal figure shows the painter's interest in creating an impression of depth in his picture.

54. (right). **Alexander of Athens. The Knucklebone Players.** Painting on marble. National Museum, Naples. Found at Herculaneum, this work, which belongs to the Roman period is generally believed to be copied from a painting of the 5th century BC. There is a skilful use of shading to render the drapery folds. The figures, which are named, are characters from Greek mythology: Leto, Niobe and Phoebe are standing, while two girls, Aglaia and Ileaira, play.

56. (above). **Scene from the frieze of Nike Temple parapet.** 421–415 BC. Marble. h. 3 ft. 5 in. (1.04 m.). Acropolis Museum, Athens. This sculptured slab comes from the parapet of the temple of the Wingless Victory on the Acropolis at Athens. The Victory, on the left, is trying to control a sacrificial bull while the one on the right takes evasive action. The sculptor here makes decorative, but rather artificial use of the discoveries made in the treatment of female drapery. Decorative work of this period was much copied in Roman times.

57. (left). **The Meidias Painter. The Rape of the Leucippids.** Late 5th century BC. Vase painting. h. (of vase) $20\frac{1}{2}$ in. (52 cm.). British Museum, London. This scene appears on a red-figure hydria by the Meidias painter. The subject is the rape of the daughters of Leucippus by the Dioscuri, Castor and Pollux. The Meidias painter who worked in the late years of the 5th century BC is noted for the same kind of decorative prettiness and charm that we see in the sculptures of the period.

58. (right). Scene on a Tarentine vase. *c.* 350 BC. Pottery. h. 9 in. (22.5 cm.). Martin von Wagner Museum, Würzburg. This fragment of a bowl, made in the south Italian Greek city of Tarentum, shows a scene from a tragedy enacted before a palace setting. The painter makes a successful, though not consistent, attempt to show the building in perspective.

59. (below). The Cyclops Painter. Early Lucanian calyx crater. *c.* 425 BC. Pottery. diam. 18 in. (45 cm.). British Museum, London. Red-figure bowl made in one of the Greek colonies of southern Italy (Lucania). The picture shows the companions of Odysseus preparing to blind Polyphemus. The arrangement of the figures shows the painter's interest in the problem of rendering spatial depth.

60. (left). **Helmeted head from Tegea.**
4th century BC. Marble. h. 6⅞ in. (17.5 cm.).
National Museum, Athens. The temple
of Athena Alea at Tegea was rebuilt after
a disaster in 394 BC; the architect is said
to have been Scopas of Paros, the famous
sculptor. This head of a warrior comes
from one of the pedimental compositions
of the temple, the subjects of which were
the Calydonian boar hunt and the battle
of Telephos and Achilles on the plain of
the *Käikos*. The style of the head is a very
individual one, which suggests the influence of a great sculptor, and it has been
taken as evidence for the work of Scopas.

61. (left). **Base of a column from the
temple of Artemis at Ephesus.** *c.* 325
BC. Marble. 5 ft. 11 in. (1.8 m.). British
Museum, London. The Old Temple of
Artemis was burnt down in 356 BC and
rebuilt on an equally grand scale in the
second half of the 4th century. The new
building was reckoned one of the Seven
Wonders of the World. The best preserved
of the massive sculptured column bases
from the temple is illustrated here. The
figures are, in the centre, Hermes, with
female draped figures on either side of him.

62. (right). **Statue of a young man
from Antikythera.** *c.* 340 BC. Bronze.
6 ft. 5 in. (1.94 m.). National Museum,
Athens. Statue of a young man found in
the sea near Antikythera, an island off the
Peloponnese. The action of the figure
seems to suggest throwing; he may have
held a ball in his right hand. The statue
has been restored from many fragments.
The eyes are inlaid with coloured glass.

63. (left). Slab of the Amazon frieze from the Mausoleum. Marble. h. 2 ft. 11 in. (89 cm.). British Museum, London. A battle between Greeks and Amazons is the subject of this best preserved of three sculptured friezes from the Mausoleum at Halicarnassus. The powerful triangular composition in the centre of the slab, consisting of an Amazon and a Greek fighting over a fallen warrior, is a recurrent motif in the design. On the left of the central group a young man is hurling a spear; on the right is a helmeted Amazon.

64. (left). The theatre at Epidaurus. *c.* 350 BC. A view of the best preserved of Greek theatres built, according to Pausanias, by the architect Polykleitos the younger. The auditorium is well preserved, the stage building ruinous. It is estimated that the theatre would hold 13,000 people; its remarkable acoustics are still a source of wonder to visitors.

65. (right). Statue of Mausolus. *c.* 350 BC. Marble. 9 ft. 4 in. (3 m.). British Museum, London. This colossal statue, found in the excavations of the Mausoleum of Halicarnassus, is generally identified as a portrait of Mausolus, prince of Caria, for whom the famous tomb was built. The figure wears Greek dress, but is characterised as an oriental by his long hair and beard.

67. (below). **Pebble Mosaic from Pella.**
c. 300 BC. Mosaic. l. 5 ft. 4¼ in. (163 cm.).
This mosaic depicts a lion hunt. Floor
mosaics appear in the Greek world in the
later 5th century BC, the earliest examples
being made of water-worn pebbles. A fine
series of pebble-mosaics has been found
recently at Pella, the birthplace of
Alexander of Macedon, dating from the
late 4th century BC. The use of cut pieces
of coloured stone (*tesserae*) for making
floor-mosaics seems to have come in
during the 3rd century BC, and superseded
the pebble technique.

66, 68. (left and right). **The Alexander Mosaic, with detail.** 1st century BC. Mosaic. h. 11 ft. 3 in. (3.42 m.). National Museum, Naples. This mosaic was found in the House of the Faun at Pompeii in 1831. The subject is the Battle of Issus (near Iskenderun), in which Alexander defeated the great King Darius of Persia. It is believed to be an accurate copy of a 4th century painting. The artist has chosen the moment when Alexander and Darius are face to face in battle. The painting is carried out in a basically four-colour scheme of red, brown, black and white applied in various tones, and shows a masterly use of foreshortening, perspective effects, and highlights. A single tree is the only landscape element in the picture. The detail on the right shows the figure of Alexander.

69. (right). **Head of a Berber.** Early Hellenistic. Bronze. h. 1 ft. (30.5 cm.). British Museum, London. This life-size head of a berber was found in the temple of Apollo at Cyrene. It may have belonged to a statue. The eyes were inset with glass. The date is uncertain, but the combination of accurate rendering of physical characteristics and a fine simplicity of form suggests the early Hellenistic period.

70. (right). **The Stoa of Attalos, Athens.**
2nd century BC. The rebuilt Stoa of Attalos
in the Agora (Market Place) at Athens.
The two story colonnade, which closed
the east side of the main square of the
Agora, was the gift of Attalos II, King of
Pergamon (159–138 BC). Its main purpose
was to provide a sheltered promenade;
each of its two stories is backed by a row
of rooms which served as shops. The combination of Doric and Ionic architecture
is typical of the Hellenistic period.

71. (below). **The Athena Group from
the frieze of the Great Altar at
Pergamon.** c. 180 BC. Marble. 7 ft. 6 in.
(2.28 m.). Staatliche Museen, East Berlin.
Part of the east frieze from the Altar of
Zeus at Pergamon, erected by Eumenes II
to commemorate the victories of his
father, Attalos I. The frieze, showing a
battle of gods and giants, was carved
round the base on which the altar stood.
In one of the best known scenes, illustrated
here, Athena is engaged in combat with
a winged giant, Alcyoneus; the earth
goddess emerges from the ground on the
right and above her is a figure of Victory
crowning Athena.

44. **Sophocles.** Roman period. Marble. h. 6 ft. 4 in. (1.93 m.). Lateran Museum. A copy of a bronze portrait statue of the great poet set up in Athens between 340 and 330 BC.

ful renderings of the human form in action. The faces show almost no expression. There is a marked contrast between the Amazon frieze and the scenes depicted on the Alexander sarcophagus (figure 46), which is latest in the series made by Greek craftsmen for the kings of Sidon, and dates from about 300 BC. The scenes of lion hunting and battle have much more of the appearance of real events. Violence and action in the bodies is accompanied by powerful expression in the faces. The figures are arranged to overlap one another, so as to give a greater impression of depth, and a skilful and realistic use of colour enhances the effect of the carving. Of course, nothing so ambitious in pictorial realism as we have seen in the Alexander mosaic (plate 66), could be attempted in sculpture but, throughout the period, new discoveries in illusionistic painting were exerting strong influence on the sculptor's art. The development of the use of landscape in painting during this time resulted in a greater use of landscape elements in the reliefs. This may be seen in the reliefs from the smaller frieze, the Telephos frieze, from the Great Altar of Zeus, built by Eumenes II at Pergamon between 180 and 160 BC. There are also a number of little reliefs with rustic scenes in landscape settings, which seem to belong to later Hellenistic times, and look very much like sculptural counterparts of panel pictures.

THE GIGANTOMACHY FRIEZE FROM PERGAMON

The battle of gods and giants, on the great frieze that decorated the Altar of Zeus at Pergamon (plate 71), is in many ways the most revealing document of Hellenistic art. It is one of the few monuments of the period inspired by stirring historical events, the victories of the Pergamene kings over the Gaulish invaders of Asia Minor, and it adopts the same allegorical method as the sculpture of 5th-century Athens to convey the triumph of Greek civilisation over barbarism. But nothing could be further from the 5th century than this highly theatrical art. The composition is a closely interwoven mass of writhing bodies, heroic and dynamic in feeling, exaggerated in gesture and expression. It is a work of immense skill and, indeed, of immense erudition. One admires these qualities without reserve, but here, as in so much of the art of the period, one senses the yearning for the grand and magnificent which leads to an overstraining of effects, and which comes from the sculptors' desire to impress with their range and skill. One longs for the simplicity and clarity of 5th-century sculpture, and it seems inevitable that this inflated and pompous art should produce, as it did, a reaction towards the more restrained styles of the 5th and 4th centuries.

THE NEO-ATTIC SCHOOL

This reaction is best exemplified by the work of the so-called Neo-Attic school, which developed in Athens during the last century BC, under the strong influence of Roman patronage. Throughout the Hellenistic period there had been a big demand for purely decorative sculpture, and this de-

45. **Ptolemy I.** *c.* 280 BC. Marble. h. 10¼ in. (26 cm.). Ny Carlsberg Glyptotek, Copenhagen. Ptolemy I, one of Alexander the Great's most trusted generals, was the founder of the dynasty of kings who ruled Egypt from 323–30 BC.

mand increased when, in the last two centuries BC, the Roman patricians became enthusiastic collectors of Greek art. There had always been a tendency to copy masterpieces of past ages, and now the Neo-Attics decided to capitalise on this aspect of contemporary taste, and produce decorative pieces in marble and other materials, making use of classical figures and themes almost purely as ornamental motifs. There is, for example, a series of relief-panels, found in the Piraeus, with scenes of Greeks and Amazons copied from the reliefs of the golden shield of Pheidias' Athena Parthenos; there is a well-head in Madrid, which seems to copy the central group representing the Birth of Athena on the east pediment of the Parthenon; there are innumerable examples of marble furniture and garden ornaments with figures based on classical and archaic models (figure 48). This Neo-Attic school exerted considerable influence on the development of art during the period of the Roman Empire; the high quality of its craftsmanship and the simplicity and clarity of its style, appealed both to the Roman patricians of the late Republic, and to those who were responsible for the decoration of public buildings in the early years of the Empire.

HELLENISTIC 'OBJETS D'ART'

As we have seen, there was not in ancient times a clear-cut distinction between the 'major' and the 'minor' arts, and in the Hellenistic period, especially, the versatile artist-craftsman was prepared to meet the demands of his patrons by working in many different media. Pasiteles of Naples, whom we have already mentioned, worked in marble, ivory, bronze, gold and silver and was famous, among other things, for his silver mirrors. Goldsmiths and silversmiths, particularly won high reputations for their products, and both rulers and private individuals built up big collections of precious metalwork. Gem-engravers produced cameos and intaglios in semi-precious stones, which were as much admired as any artistic products of the period. The *Tazza Farnese*, a sardonyx cup decorated with an elaborate Egyptian allegory (plate 78), is one of the finest examples of Hellenistic gem carving that has come down to us, the work perhaps of an Egyptian artist at the court of the Ptolemies. The output of the silversmiths included bowls ornamented with portrait medallions, cups decorated with elaborate figured scenes (figure 63), and ornaments of different kinds, all of which were the products of educated and highly skilled craftsmanship. As in all other branches of art, the Romans inherited this Hellenistic taste for 'objets d'art', and paid enormous prices for them in the last century BC.

THE DEVELOPMENT OF PAINTING

There is very little direct evidence for the development of painting in Hellenistic times. The art of vase-painting declined during the 4th century and had practically ceased by the end of it, and there are almost no surviving wall paintings or panel pictures. In the earlier chapters we have tried to trace the general lines of the development of illusionistic painting. By the late 4th century, painters, if we may judge from the written record and the evidence of the Alexander mosaic, while still using a comparatively limited palette, had mastered the techniques of modelling in colour, and had made great advances in the handling of pictorial space and in the understanding of linear and aerial perspective. The Hellenistic age further developed these techniques, and vastly extended the subject matter of the art of painting. The admiration for illusionistic tricks in the work of 4th-century painters leads Hellenistic painters to experiment with new methods of 'trompe l'œil'. Experiments in per-

46. **The Alexander Sarcophagus.** Late 4th century BC. Marble. h. 6 ft. 4¾ in. (1.95 m.). Archaeological Museum, Istanbul. One of a series of sculptured marble coffins by Greek artists, found in the royal necropolis of Sidon in Syria. The scene shows Alexander out hunting. The reliefs were richly painted.

47. **Bull's head capital.** 3rd century BC. Marble. h. 3 ft. 3 in. (1 m.). British Museum, London. Capital decorated with bulls' heads, found at Salamis in Cyprus. The design combines Greek and Persian elements.

spective inspired a scientific enquiry into its principles, and in late Hellenistic times, Greek painting seems to have achieved something very close to a consistent theory of linear perspective.

The pebble floor mosaics recently discovered at Pella, the birthplace of Alexander the Great, date from the late 4th century BC. Like all early Greek mosaics, they are composed of natural pebbles of a comparatively small range of colours. The lion-hunt scene, shown in plate 67, shows a limited use of chiaroscuro in the modelling of the bodies and drapery, but probably gives very little idea of what had already been achieved in painting. In the series of painted tombstones from Pagasai in North Greece, there is evidence of further advances in technique, especially in the wider use of mixed colours and in the treatment of depth. The figures in the background are shown in smaller scale, and there is even some suggestion of aerial perspective in the colour-tones used for more distant features. But apart from very few examples such as these, our evidence for the great advances in painting made during the Hellenistic period is drawn from surviving works of the 1st century BC and the 1st century AD. With few exceptions, these paintings derive from the interior decoration of Roman houses, especially at Pompeii and the other towns of the Bay of Naples which were buried by the eruption of Vesuvius in AD 79.

ROMAN COPIES OF HELLENISTIC PAINTINGS

The use of these paintings as evidence for the development of Hellenistic art requires some explanation. By the 2nd century BC, the interior decoration of Greek private houses had become quite luxurious. Furnishings were more elaborate, the walls were decorated with paintings and the floors with mosaics. The latter were now carried out in a new

technique—the use of small cut stones of many colours instead of the natural pebbles. The new technique made possible rich polychrome effects, such as we see in 2nd- and 1st-century floors at Delos, and mosaics could be closely copied from paintings.

HELLENISTIC WALL-DECORATION

The earliest style of Hellenistic painted wall-decoration is a simple one, imitating the use of facings of coloured marble, which apparently decorated the interior of the palaces and houses of the very wealthy. This style of interior decoration is widespread in the Hellenistic world, and it reached Italy in the late 2nd century BC; at Pompeii, where it is known as the 'First Style', it prevailed down to about 80 BC. The walls are divided up into three zones—a dado, a wide central zone, and a crowning entablature. Painting is combined with stucco relief, to give the impression of real masonry construction. The style which superseded this relies entirely on the use of paint to create illusionistic effects; it still retains the basically triple division of the wall, but the central section is much more elaborately decorated. The basic element of design is usually a row of widely spaced columns or pilasters in the foreground, painted to look like real architectural features; behind these columns the artist tries to give an impression of an architectural vista, or a landscape, or a scene with figures. These schemes owe their success to a fine command of the principles of illusionistic painting. Although almost all the surviving examples of the 'Second Style' are from Italy, there are one or two from other parts of the Hellenistic world, and it seems clear that the style was invented in Greece and brought to Italy by Greek artists and craftsmen.

The Second Style wall-decorations in Italy, and those of the subsequent Pompeian styles which are discussed in the

48. **The Medici Vase.** 1st century BC. Marble. h. 5 ft. 8 in. (1.73 m.). Uffizi Gallery, Florence. A typical product of the Neo-Attic school, this vase is decorated with reliefs depicting a scene from Greek mythology, perhaps the sacrifice of Iphigeneia.

last chapter, introduce us to almost every *genre* of painting. There is still life, portraiture, landscape with figures, nature-painting, scenes of everyday life, apart from the traditional mythological figure-scenes that had long been part of the repertoire of Greek painting. It seems certain that the techniques and range of subjects employed by the interior decorators of Pompeii, and elsewhere in Italy, were discovered in the Hellenistic period. The literary sources make it fairly clear that all these *genres* were practised by Hellenistic painters, and it is a fair assumption that in many cases we are seeing copies of their work. Some of the big pictures incorporated in decorative schemes are probably close copies of famous masterpieces of the 4th century and later; others are free adaptations.

THE ODYSSEY LANDSCAPES

Three famous Second Style wall-paintings are illustrated here in plates 79–81. The first of these, the *Odyssey Landscape* (plate 80), which once decorated the wall of a house on the Esquiline Hill in Rome, illustrates a scene from the adven-

tures of Odysseus as told in Homer's poem, and was painted about 50 BC. Landscape, as we have seen, had played little part in classical painting; the setting for the scene was indicated by a few 'symbolic' rocks and trees, which are dominated by the figures. In the 4th century there is evidence for an increasingly significant use of landscape detail, but its role remains strictly subordinate. In the Odyssey picture, on the other hand, the landscape dominates the figures, and the painter shows his delight in portraying the world of nature for itself. This development of the art of nature painting belongs to the Hellenistic world, and we can judge from this example how far Hellenistic artists had advanced. They have not completely succeeded in creating a unified landscape illumined by a single source of light and seen from a single viewpoint. There is no suggestion of a single perspective system in the picture, but it is remarkable how skilfully the artist contrives to show atmospheric effects, how cleverly he relates the figures to the landscape, and suggests the effect of distance by subtle modifications in the colours of the distant objects.

ARCHITECTURAL PAINTING

The second of the pictures shows an architectural wall from a villa at Boscoreale (plate 81). Behind the foreground columns, the painter opens up a vista of elaborate architecture receding into the background. The advances made by Greek artists in showing buildings and other objects in recession were, so far as we can judge from our sources, associated with scene-painting for the theatre. A view of the king's palace commonly formed the backcloth for tragic plays, private houses for comedy, a country scene for satyr-plays, and it was natural that the scene-painters should attempt to make this background as realistic as possible. Our picture probably shows such a theatrical stage-setting, and we can see how closely the painter has come to giving the picture a consistent linear perspective, in which all the parallel lines recede to a single vanishing point. There seems little doubt that Hellenistic artists had developed, by experiment and study, a system of perspective. In the Second-Style paintings from Pompeii, and elsewhere, one sees evidence for this Hellenistic discovery but, curiously, its use is short-lived. Later Roman wall-paintings ignore it, reverting to a multiplicity of vanishing points within the same composition, where each object has its own foreshortening unrelated to that of neighbouring objects. Nor are individual objects consistently foreshortened. It was not until the Renaissance that the principles of perspective were again understood completely by painters.

THE VILLA OF THE MYSTERIES

The third of our pictures (plate 79) illustrates part of the famous Dionysiac initiation scenes on a Second-Style wall in the so-called Villa of the Mysteries, at Pompeii. The central portion of the wall shows a continuous frieze of figures against a background of pilasters, the subject of which is the initiation of a young woman into the mystery-rites of the Dionysiac cult. There is no attempt here at elaborate illusionistic effects; the scenes are represented against a red background, the interest entirely concentrated on the movement and expression of the figures. But in the treatment of the bodies and faces there is remarkable skill in modelling with colour, which enables the painter to give a very convincing rendering of this dramatic subject. There are paintings in very similar style, from a villa found at Boscoreale, with portraits of philosophers and famous figures which are believed to be copied from court-paintings of the 3rd century BC.

MOSAICS OF THE FIRST CENTURY BC

The wide range of subjects in Hellenistic painting is illustrated by some of the mosaic panels from 2nd- and 1st-century floors at Pompeii. These panels are among the finest examples of mosaic work that have survived from the ancient world; the technique of using very small pieces of coloured stone, with a wide range of colours, enables the mosaicist to imitate the effects of painting fairly closely. One of these mosaics, the *Alexander Mosaic* from the House of the Faun at Pompeii, has already been mentioned as giving a good idea of a lost masterpiece of the 4th century BC. Other subjects are landscape scenes, compositions of marine life and *genre* scenes, like the well-known mosaic of the street musicians from Herculaneum, signed by a Greek craftsman Dioscourides (plate 82). Other popular subjects go back to the work of Sosus, an artist of the Pergamene school, who seems to have specialised in 'trompe l'œil'. One of these shows doves drinking from a bowl of water, and was admired clearly for the remarkable illusion of reality that the artist managed to convey (plate 83). His most famous piece of 'trompe l'œil', was the picture of the 'unswept floor' which had as its theme the remnants of food cast on the floor by diners at a banquet. A copy of this work has been found in Rome.

HELLENISTIC ARCHITECTURE AND TOWN-PLANNING

These Roman paintings and mosaics compensate, to some extent, for the almost complete lack of original works of Hellenistic painting. The conclusions drawn from the study of them are similar to those we have observed in the account of Hellenistic sculpture—a search for new themes and rapid development of new techniques and methods. The third of the major arts, that of architecture, illustrates perhaps best of all the chief contribution of the Hellenistic period to the history of art. As we have seen, Greek architecture of the classical period had achieved perfection in a few traditional forms of building. The perfect Doric temple was the Parthenon, and no Doric temple thereafter could surpass it, or even compare with it. The Hellenistic world was not concerned with perfection, though it produced its crop of academic architects, who laid down precise and unchangeable rules of architectural form, which they tried to follow in their buildings. This academic 'classicism' is a very small part of the Hellenistic achievement. The Greek world after Alexander saw the foundation of many new towns and cities over a wide area, and all the varied aspects of city life were now the concern of the architects and planners. The cities were laid out in regular plans in accordance with rules of town-planning developed in the 5th century BC. We have already drawn attention to the contrast between the splendour of the temples of the gods in the old city-states and the haphazard and even squalid domestic quarters. The contrasts were far less marked in Hellenistic cities; houses were laid out in regularly planned areas defined by crossing streets; attention was paid to public hygiene and the comforts of private life. Hellenistic homes were often large and spacious, and richly decorated inside; the palaces of rulers were incomparably grand in planning and architecture. The varied activities of public life were catered for by well-designed buildings of permanent character. There had been no stone theatre in the Greek world until the 4th century, but in the Hellenistic period every Greek city had its permanent theatre, and many had concert halls and other places of public entertainment. Stone-built *stadia* for athletic events were associated with the gymnasium which was the city's centre for athletic exercise and, indeed, the hub of the whole educational system. Around the market-place, which was the political as well as the commercial centre of city-life, there were shady colonnades where people could meet and talk, as well as the permanent buildings of the city's political life—the council chamber and the assembly hall. The temples of the gods were still built on a grand scale, and still dominated the layout of the cities; some were designed on a scale that completely overshadowed the great buildings of the city-states.

PERGAMON UNDER THE ATTALIDS

The buildings of the main capitals of the Hellenistic world are not well-known to us. The only Hellenistic city that gives us a good picture of the magnificence of public building is Pergamon where, as we have seen, during the 3rd and 2nd centuries the Attalid dynasty spent lavishly on buildings and works of art, to adorn their capital. The Acropolis of Pergamon is still a monument to their ostentation. Of the sculptures of the Great Altar of Zeus, with its enormous columned enclosure built round the altar of the god, we have already spoken. Only the foundations of the altar remain today, but we can still get a good impression of the great scale of the other buildings on the Acropolis, of the palace of the kings, the library, the porticos, and the enormous theatre built against the slope of the rock. It is significant that the legacy of the last of the Attalid kings, by which he bequeathed his kingdom to the Romans in 133 BC, gave the new world conquerors their first permanent foothold in Asia, and that new conceptions of monumental building on a grand scale came very shortly afterwards to Italy.

NEW METHODS OF CONSTRUCTION

Generally speaking, the traditional methods of building and forms of decoration continued to be practised in Hellenistic times. There was no revolution in techniques, such as we find at the beginning of the Roman period, but a number of new building methods began to make their appearance. The most important is the arch, constructed of a series of wedge-shaped stones, called voussoirs, which was to become a basic constructional form of Roman architecture. In Hellenistic times the arch did not replace the column and lintel method of spanning a space, but there were already a number of very assured examples of its use in the last two centuries BC, and the probability is that the arch was an invention of Hellenistic architects.

THE TREATMENT OF THE 'ORDERS'

The development of the classical 'orders' of architecture during Hellenistic times, is typical of the character of the age. As we have seen, only the Doric order had achieved its complete 'canonical' form by the middle of the 5th century;

the details of the Ionic still varied from place to place, and the Corinthian had scarcely made its appearance. In the hands of Hellenistic architects the Doric began to lose its uncompromising rigidity of form. The precise rules for fluting the column, for forming the capitals, for spacing the triglyphs of the frieze, are often ignored; the proportions became more slender and light. The Ionic comes more and more into favour, and acquires an established form combining frieze and dentils on the cornice; different varieties of capital are used in different places, a developed form with volutes at the corners being especially popular in the Greek colonies of southern Italy. The Corinthian, admired as it was for its richer decorative qualities, comes into its own. In Athens about 170 BC, Antiochus IV of Syria resumed the building of the enormous Temple of Olympian Zeus, and gave us the earliest example of Corinthian architecture on a grand scale. No new form of entablature was invented for this new order; Corinthian capitals were combined with the developed version of the Ionic.

Combinations of the orders, which would surely have shocked the taste of classical architects, came into fashion. In the colonnade or *stoa* of Attalos II, which has now been reconstructed in the Agora at Athens, the architecture of the ground floor is Doric, that of the upper floor is Ionic, and a very unorthodox Ionic at that (plate 70). Hellenistic unorthodoxy went even further by combining elements of the different orders into a single scheme; Ionic columns are found with Doric superstructure, Corinthian columns with Doric and Ionic. More significant perhaps for the future history of architecture, is the increasing tendency towards the purely decorative use of architectural forms that have an essentially structural origin. Engaged columns and pilasters, serving purely as decoration of a wall-surface, pave the way for the Roman use of applied orders in conjunction with arch and concrete construction, such as we see in the great buildings of the Roman Empire (see plate 113).

HELLENISTIC ART

The Hellenistic period is a vital stage in the history of European art. The basic discoveries of the Greeks of the 5th and 4th centuries were developed and extended, artistic techniques were fully worked out and applied. The age gave to the world a new conception of art as a manifestation of human life in all its varied aspects; art descends from its Olympian heights into everyday life. In so doing it loses much; the great periods of art have been inspired by limited ideals, and by its very range Hellenistic art falls short of greatness. Hellenistic art can be pretty and eloquent by turns; it can be pleasing and winning, but when it tries to be grand it is usually grandiose. But the gains surely outweigh the losses; for the first time in history men saw clearly that art does have a role to play in every part of life.

Greek artists outside the Greek World and the Art of the Etruscans

The chapter of this book which discusses the origins of Greek art, stressed the foreign contribution to the tradition. Here we are concerned with the influence of Greek art among the non-Greek peoples who were their neighbours. In one special case, that of the Etruscans in central Italy, to whom most of this chapter is mainly devoted, we are dealing with a subject which is central to our theme—the development of the Greek tradition—because Etruscan art forms the background to the art of the Romans. Before the latter came to a position of power, which eventually enabled them to create a great empire, Greek art had won enthusiastic acceptance in the cities of Etruria; without this background of Hellenised Etruscan art, it is doubtful whether Rome would ever have adopted Greek art as she did, and it is certain that the character of Roman art would have been far different.

GREEK EXPORTS

From the 7th century BC onwards, Greek works of art were widely exported outside the Greek world. Geometric and 'orientalising' pottery was traded over the Mediterranean, and came into the hands of barbarians. In the 6th century the volume of trade was vastly increased, and the peoples of central Europe began to know and value Greek pottery and metalwork. We have already mentioned the famous crater of Vix, perhaps the finest Greek bronze vessel that has come down to us (plate 41). This was found in a chieftain's grave at Vix, in central France. The Thracian tribes on the northern frontier of the Greek world were using Greek metal vessels from the middle of the 6th century BC, as were the Scythian neighbours of the Greek colonies on the Black Sea. The Iron Age peoples of Italy were ardent collectors of Greek objects. By means of archaeological discoveries Greek commerce can be followed from Marseilles up the Rhône valley and into the heart of Switzerland.

GREEK ARTISTS ABROAD

From the early 6th century, Greek artists and craftsmen seem to have lent their services to their non-Greek neighbours. As we shall see, in the middle of the 6th century immigrant craftsmen from Ionia set up workshops to produce pottery in Etruria. Greeks were making objects to the local taste of Scythians and Thracians in the same period. Wall paintings in pure Greek style of the late 6th century have been found at Gordion, in Phrygia. The Persians called for Greek artists to work on the grandiose building-schemes of Darius and Xerxes at Persepolis, and elsewhere; the stone friezes from the palace of Persepolis show us an art which is non-Greek in spirit, yet adopts many of the conventions of Greek art in the treatment of drapery, hair and other details (plate 45). We hear, in fact, of a certain Greek artist, by name Telephanes, who spent his entire career in the employ of Darius and Xerxes. The ruling house of Sidon, from the early 5th century onwards, certainly had Greek artists to carve the sarcophagi in which they were buried; the earliest examples have the anthropoid form traditional in Egyptian coffins, but the heads are often carved in purely Greek style. Figure 49 shows one of the 'Greek' anthropoid sarcophagi from Sidon, side by side with one in Egyptian style. The Persian satraps in Asia Minor employed Greek artists throughout the 5th century and in the 4th. The Nereid monument at Xanthus, erected in the early 4th century, is one of many grand funerary monuments made by Greeks for foreign dynasts; the grandest of all was the famous Mausoleum, the tomb of Mausolus, prince of Caria around 350 BC, a building in which all the most famous sculptors of the day were said to have worked, and which was counted among the Seven Wonders of the World.

THE INFLUENCE OF GREEK ART ABROAD

Thus, long before Alexander's conquests hellenised the entire known world, Greek artists and Greek works of art had reached far afield. From our point of view, the chief interest in this penetration lies in its permanent effects upon the arts of the areas it affected. These effects range from poor imitation of imported works to the creative adaptation of Greek ideas into an independent living tradition. It is not possible yet to assess fully all the effects, because of the difficulties in dating much of the material that has come down to us. It is easy to see similarities, some perhaps fortuitous, between early Indian sculptures and 6th-century *kouroi*, between seated Buddhas and Ionian figures, between Celto-Ligurian sculptures from Provence and late archaic Greek sculpture, but we are still far from understanding the precise relationship between them. In some cases we are on firmer ground. We can follow the influence of Greek art on the essentially non-representational artistic traditions of the Scythians and the Celts. We can see how the early Iberian bronze sculptures in Spain derive from a mixed tradition of local, oriental and Greek elements. The influence of Greek 5th-century sculpture is very strong in the stone sculptures from Iberian sites as, for example, in the well-known figure of the 'High Priestess' from Cerro de los Santos (figure 51), or the famous Elche bust, both of which owe much to Greek art, although the ideas that inspired them are non-Greek.

GREEK ART AND THE ETRUSCANS

These early influences of Greek art outside the Greek world paved the way for the progressive 'Hellenisation' of the European world after Alexander. In all these cases, Greek ideals, imperfectly understood, are seen working on and modifying local traditions; in some cases, they provide the main stimulus for the creation of a representational art where none had existed before. Etruria provides us with

49. **Anthropoid Sarcophagi.** *c.* 460 BC. Archaeological Museum, Istanbul. Two anthropoid sarcophagi found in the royal necropolis at Sidon in Syria. The form of the coffins is Egyptian, but the heads are carved in Greek style and by Greek artists.

50. **Lycian Sarcophagus.** Late 5th century BC. h. 9 ft. 8¾ in. (2.96 m.). Archaeological Museum, Istanbul. The sarcophagus from the royal necropolis at Sidon with its high, pyramidal cover, is in the form of a Lycian tomb. The reliefs, which show hunting scenes, are in Greek style.

the special case of an area where, from a very early period, we can follow out the development of an artistic tradition heavily indebted to Greek inspiration, yet showing at all times a certain independence. Many have held the view that Etruscan art is no more than inferior imitation of Greek art, and there is, indeed, some truth in this view. The Etruscans coveted the products of Greek artists and craftsmen, and imported them in enormous quantities. In the early 19th century, Greek red-figured vases were commonly known as Etruscan, because so many of them had been found in the tombs of wealthy Etruscans. From the late 7th century onwards, Greek art provided the main stimulus for art in Etruria, and almost all the products of Etruscan art may be recognised as more or less derivative from the art of the Greeks. And yet there are qualities in the best Etruscan art which raise it far above a purely 'provincial' status, making it worthy of study for itself. Furthermore, as we have already mentioned, the art of the Etruscans provides a vital link in the chain of historical continuity between Greek and Roman art, without which it is impossible to understand the development of the classical tradition in the Roman world. Finally, it should be said that there are those who see in the character of Etruscan representational art, from a very early period, the same anti-classical elements that modify and eventually transform the classical tradition in the late Roman Empire.

ETRUSCAN ART AND THE PROBLEM
OF THEIR ORIGINS

We are not here concerned with the vexed question of the origins of the Etruscans, except in so far as it affects the character of their art. The Etruscan problem has been argued out in terms of the two conflicting ancient accounts of their origins, the more widely accepted view being that they were an immigrant people from Asia Minor arriving in Italy some time after the period of the Trojan War. A later view, still held by many today, is that they were a people indigenous to Italy. In their art and architecture we shall find evidence that seems to support now the one, now the other hypothesis, but it is dangerous evidence to handle. In the case of a people so receptive to foreign art as the Etruscans, a new artistic influence has no bearing on the problem of their ethnic formation. It is now generally agreed, for example, that the strongly orientalising phase of Etruscan art in the 7th century BC is no more evidence for the oriental origin of the people than is the similar orientalising phase we have observed in Greek art. This is not to say that a deeper understanding of Etruscan art will not, in the end, throw light upon their origins, but we shall find the evidence, if anywhere, in the differences between their art and its oriental and Greek models rather than in its similarities. One factor which comes out clearly in their art is a strongly indigenous element; there seems to be a

(Continued on page 121)

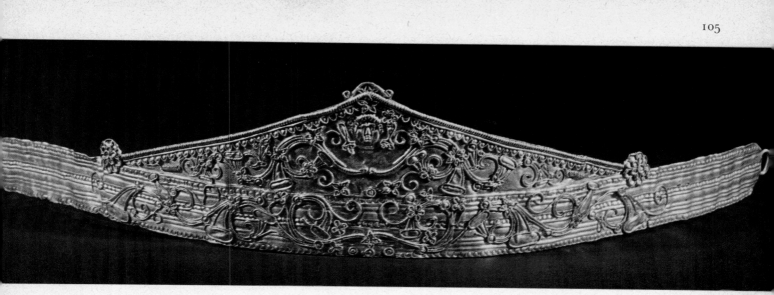

72. (above). **Decorated diadem.** 3rd century BC. Gold. 1⅝ in. (4.2 cm.). British Museum, London. Diadem found at St. Eufemia del Golfo near Monteleone in south Italy. The diadem is decorated with tendrils and flowers of filigree work; near the apex of the triangle is a little embossed head. The floral ornament is typical of south Italian decorative work in the Hellenistic period.

73. (below). **Conversation piece.** *c.* 200 BC. Terracotta. h. 8 in. (20 cm.). British Museum, London. This little painted terracotta group shows two women sitting on a couch talking to one another; the elder woman on the right is perhaps giving advice to the younger. A pleasant everyday theme of a kind that the makers of terracotta figures liked to portray in Hellenistic times. The group probably comes from Myrina in Asia Minor.

74. (right). **Aphrodite, Pan and Eros.**
c. 100 BC. Marble. 4 ft. 4 in. (1.32 m.).
National Museum, Athens. A group made
for a Syrian merchant on the island of
Delos. Aphrodite is warding off Pan's
attack with a sandal, while Eros grabs
Pan's horn in order to push him away.
The group is a good example of a large
series of light-hearted groups of satyrs,
Pans, centaurs and so on, which were
made to satisfy a taste for decorative
sculpture in Hellenistic times.

75. (below). **Head vase.** *c.* 100 BC. Bronze
h. 4 in. (10 cm.). British Museum, London.
Little jug cast in the form of a negress's
head. Silver inlay is used for the whites of
the eyes. The negroid features are closely
observed but not exaggerated; the fashion
for corkscrew curls still prevails among
some African tribes today. The vase was
probably made in the late Hellenistic period.

76. (below). **Tetradrachm of Antimachus of Bactria.** *c.* 175 BC. Silver.
d. 1¼ in. (3 cm.). British Museum, London.
The kingdom of Bactria declared its independence from the Seleucids in Syria
in 208 BC, and flourished for over 100
years. The portrait heads of the kings of
the dynasty on their coinage are the work
of first-class Greek artists.

77. (right). **Portrait head of a man
from Delos.** *c.* 100 BC. Bronze. 13 in.
(33 cm.). National Museum, Athens.
It is one of the best examples in the series
of portraits, in marble and bronze, of
merchants and officials made in the last
two centuries BC on the commercial island
of Delos. The eyes are of glass inlay.

78. (left). **The Tazza Farnese.** 2nd or 1st century BC. Sardonyx. diam. 8 in. (20 cm.). National Museum, Naples. The scene on the inside of this shallow cup is an allegory of the fertility of Egypt. A figure representing the Nile is seated on the left; below him is Euthenia, goddess of prosperity, resting against a sphinx. Triptolemus, bringer of fertility, is in the centre; to the right are two graceful female figures, and two youthful wind-gods float across the scene above. On the outside of the cup is a superbly carved Medusa head. The cup was probably made in Ptolemaic Egypt in the 2nd or 1st century BC.

79. (left). **Pompeian wall painting.** *c.* 50 BC. Fresco. Villa of the Mysteries, Pompeii. Detail from the famous painted frieze showing the initiation rites of the Bacchic mystery. Silenus, the attendant of Bacchus, appears with two other satyrs; on the back wall to the left a woman, her veil caught by the wind, is moving rapidly away. The painting belongs to the so-called Second Style.

80. (right). **The Odyssey landscape.** 50–30 BC. Fresco. 4 ft. 11 in. (1.50 m.). The Vatican Library. This picture is one of a series of paintings decorating a 'Second Style' wall scheme, found in a Roman house on the Esquiline Hill, Rome, and now in the Vatican. It illustrates one of Odysseus' adventures in the land of the Laestrygonians; the men who have been sent by Odysseus meet the king's daughter, who is coming down to draw water at a spring. The artist has conjured up a fairy tale landscape of cliffs and rocks and trees. The skilful handling of light, shade and colour, and the way in which the figures are fitted into the landscape, show how far Hellenistic artists had advanced in illusionistic painting.

81. (right). **Wall painting from a Villa at Boscoreale.** *c.* 50 BC. Fresco. l. 4 ft. 9 in. (1.45 m.). National Museum, Naples. Painted wall of the so-called 'Second-Style' from the dining-room of a villa at Boscoreale in the Bay of Naples. The architectural vista may be based upon the design of a Greek stage set of the Hellenistic period. It is noteworthy that in general the parallel lines of the composition recede to a single vanishing point suggesting that the painter understood the essentials of a theory of perspective. It is only in these 'Second Style' paintings that this kind of consistency is achieved. The lighting of the architecture is arbitrary, that is, there is no single uniform source of light.

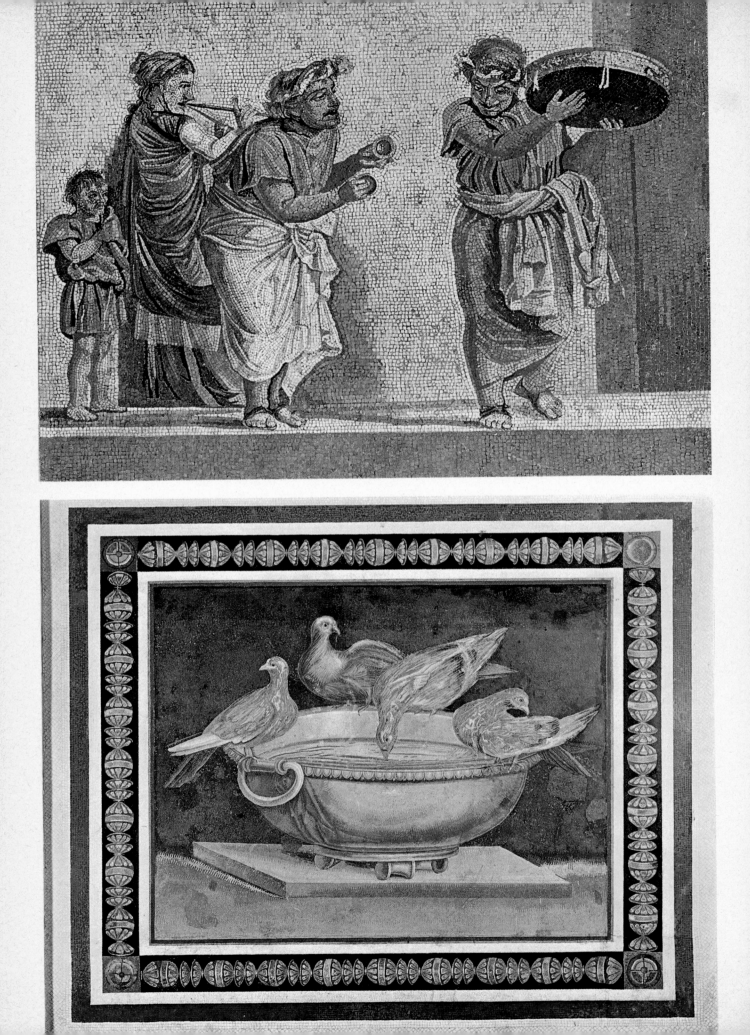

82. (left). **Dioscourides of Samos. Musicians.** *c.* 3rd century BC. Mosaic. h. 16⅛ in. (41 cm.). National Museum, Naples. This mosaic, from the so-called Villa of Cicero at Pompeii, is signed by the artist, who also signed a second mosaic in the house showing a scene from the Greek New Comedy. This one is a fine example of the mosaicist's skill in handling minute pieces of coloured stone to imitate the effects of painting; it was probably copied from a Hellenistic painting, perhaps of the 3rd century BC.

83. (left). **Doves around a bowl.** 2nd century AD. Mosaic. h. 2 ft. 9½ in. (85 cm.). Capitoline Museum, Rome. This mosaic, from the Villa of Hadrian at Tivoli, is probably a copy of a mosaic by Sosus of Pergamon (2nd century BC), which is described by Pliny the Elder as showing a dove drinking from a vessel while other doves are perched on the rim. There is another version of the same theme in Naples.

84. (right). **Figure of seated woman from Cerveteri.** 7th century BC. Terracotta. h. 21½ in. (54 cm.). British Museum, London. Figure of a seated figure from Caere (Cerveteri). This figure, together with another similar one and a seated figure of a man, was found in a chamber tomb and probably represented the family of the dead. The right hand is held out to receive an offering. The cloak is pinned to the right shoulder with one of those elaborate *fibulae*, of which examples survive in gold and other materials. The figure was made in the 7th century, when there was strong oriental influence on the art of Etruria.

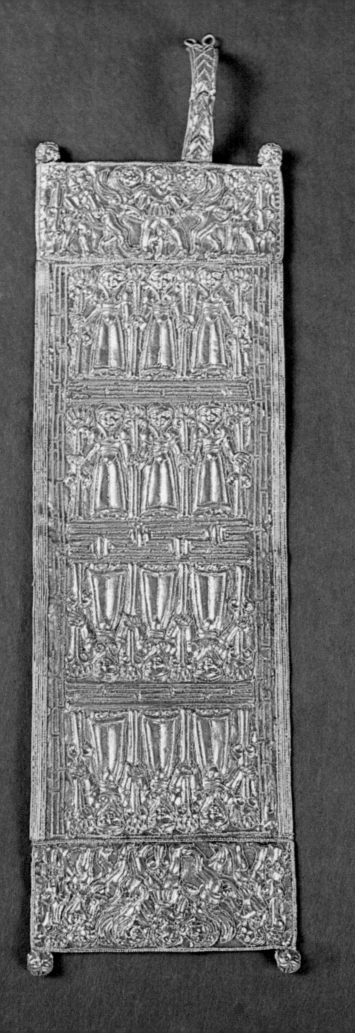

85. (left). **Bracelet from Praeneste.**
Gold. l. 7¼ in. (18.3 cm.). British Museum,
London. This bracelet is made from a
sheet of gold decorated with repoussé
figures, to which details are added in the
granulation technique. The figures belong
to an 'orientalising' repertory; there are
winged lions, male figures and rows of
female figures. Clasps and hooks are fitted
to the ends of the bracelet.

87. (right). **Cup with sphinxes from
the Bernardini tomb, Praeneste.**
7th century BC. Gold. 3⅛ in. (7.9 cm.).
Villa Giulia Museum, Rome. The Etruscan goldsmith has placed two little
sphinxes made of sheet gold decorated
with gold granulation, on each of the
handles of the cup which is a typical
7th century Greek shape.

86. (below). **Etruscan ornament from the Barberini tomb, Praeneste.** Gold. 9⅝ in. (24.3 cm.). Villa Giulia Museum, Rome. The 7th century tombs of Etruria and Latium testify to the great wealth of the Etruscan lords of the period. Gold jewellery and vessels of precious metal are among the richest that have come down to us from the ancient world. This gold ornament has little figures of lions, sphinxes, and griffins soldered on to gold sheet. The figures are embossed and decorated with lines of minute gold granules, a technique which is characteristic of the jewellery of the period.

88. (above). **The ambush of Troilus.**
c. 540 BC. Fresco. w. 4 ft. 2 in. (127 cm.).
Tomb of the Bulls, Tarquinia. The Trojan
prince Troilus, son of Priam, whose horse
can just be seen on the right of this detail,
is coming down to a well to water his
horse. Achilles is just about to sally forth

from hiding and kill him. This picture is
one of the oldest in the series of tomb
paintings from Tarquinia. The inspiration
is drawn from Greek vases, but the use
of trees and bushes suggesting a landscape
setting is in Etruscan taste.

89. (below). **A chariot race.** *c.* 450 BC.
Fresco. w. 4 ft. 10 in. (148 cm.). Tomb of
the Colle Casuccini, Chiusi. Scenes connected with the games are among the
most popular subjects in early Etruscan
tomb paintings. This picture is one of the
liveliest examples that has survived.

90. (below). **The blinding of Polyphemus.** *c.* 530–510 BC. Pottery. h. 17½ in. (44 cm). Villa Guilia Museum, Rome. The blinding of Polyphemus by Odysseus and his companions is the subject of the painting on this hydria found at Caere. Three men are driving the stake into the Cyclops' eye, while a fourth urges them on. The vase is one of the so-called Caeretan hydriae (water pots), a group of some thirty black-figure vessels, most of which have been found at Caere in Etruria. They were probably made in a single workshop at Caere by a Greek immigrant from Ionia.

91. (above). **Musicians from the Tomb
of the Leopards.** *c.* 480–470 BC. Fresco.
h. 3 ft. 6 in. (106 cm.). Etruscan Necropolis, Tarquinia. Painted scene from the
Tomb of the Leopards at Tarquinia.
On the left a young man holding a cup,
in the centre a man playing a double pipe,
and on the right a man playing a lyre.
The scene is typical of the gay, colourful
paintings of the early tombs at Tarquinia
in a style which is basically archaic Greek.
Laurel bushes are set between the figures.

92. (left). **Etruscan Banqueter.** *c.* 500
BC. Bronze. l. 13¼ in. (33 cm.). British
Museum, London. The figure, perhaps a
satyr, is reclining on a wineskin (?).
He holds a dish in his right hand. The
forms of the body are strangely elongated.

93. (right). **The Apollo of Veii.** *c.* 500 BC.
Terracotta. 5 ft. 9 in. (1.75 m.). Villa
Guilia Museum, Rome. This figure is
perhaps the most famous of all Etruscan
sculptures. It belongs to a group representing Hercules' theft of the holy hind
of the god Apollo at Delphi, which decorated an Etruscan Temple at Veii.
Though based on Greek models the figure
has an individual character that is un-
mistakably Etruscan.

94. (below). **The Nazzano Painter. Calyx crater.** *c.* 400–350 BC. Pottery. h. 22½ in. (51 cm.). Villa Giulia Museum, Rome. This red-figure vase, depicting the sack of Troy, was made at Falerii (Città Castellana). The scene has the lively con- fusion of a burlesque, perhaps an inten- tional one. King Priam lies on the ground with a warrior standing threateningly over him; on the left Aphrodite is protecting Helen from the wrath of Menelaus. Neoptolemus is brandishing the boy Astyanax by the leg.

95. (above). **An Etruscan funeral banquet.** 3rd century BC. Fresco. h. 4 ft. 8 in. (142 cm.). Tomb of the Shields, Tarquinia. In this scene the dead man, Larth Velcha, is shown with his wife, Velia Seitithi, in a melancholy scene that contrasts strongly with the festive gaiety of earlier Etruscan tomb paintings. Larth Velcha lived in the 3rd century BC, and held high rank in the priesthood. His head suggests a convincing portrait, and the intensity of his expression has something in common with Roman portraits of the 3rd century AD.

96. (below). **Sarcophagus of the Amazons from Tarquinia.** *c.* 350 BC. Alabaster. h. 20¼ in. (51 cm.). Archaeological Museum, Florence. This scene, on a painted sarcophagus in Florence, shows a chariot driven by Amazons. The figures are drawn in outline, with a clever use of shading to give an impression of three-dimensional form. Different tones of colour are used for effects of light and shade on the chariot. Perspective and foreshortening are skilfully handled. The sarcophagus was found at Tarquinia, but it is suggested that it was painted by a south Italian Greek.

97. **Portrait of Velia.** Late 4th century BC. Fresco. h. 16⅛ in. (41 cm.). Etruscan Necropolis, Tarquinia. This head of Velia, wife of Arnth Velcha comes from the Tomb of Orcus at Tarquinia. She wears a wreath of leaves and rich jewellery. The head is closely inspired by Greek art of the 4th century BC. The profile is beautifully drawn, and there is a subtle use of colour tones in the modelling of the face.

clear, unbroken line of development from the 'canopic' jars of northern Etruria, where a carefully modelled head dominates a summarily rendered body, to the late Etruscan portrait effigies on stone and terracotta sarcophagi. There is a continuity of ideas from the clay hut-urns of the Villanovans in southern Etruria and Latium to the most elaborate house-tomb structures of the Etruscans. There are perhaps more subtle implications to be drawn from the obvious Etruscan delight in representing the world of nature, a delight that seems to bring us closer to the Minoans, and the Egyptians, among the peoples of the Mediterranean, and from their essential failure to understand the ideals of Greek art and culture.

THE DEVELOPMENT OF ETRUSCAN POWER

Leaving aside the problems of the Etruscans as a people, and the contribution that the study of their art may make to these problems, we must attempt a brief archaeological and historical survey of Etruria as a prelude to considering their art. In the 8th century BC there are clear signs of the development in the Etruscan area of a culture distinct from the rest of Iron Age Italy, a development which is accompanied by a considerable accession of wealth and new burial customs. There are inscriptions in the Etruscan language, a language which has no basic affinity with the Indo-European languages of Italy, as early as the middle of the 7th century. In southern Etruria a very rich orientalising phase, represented by the lordly burials in the Regolini-Galassi tomb at Caere and elsewhere, characterises the 7th century. A rapid development of art and civilisation, though not everywhere on the same pattern, may be observed in all the centres which later became famous as Etruscan cities—Veii, Tarquinia, Vulci, Chiusi and the rest. By about 500 BC Etruria had come to the height of her power. A federation of the principal city-states of Etruria had expanded Etruscan power northwards into the Po valley, and southwards into Campania. The Etruscans were trading widely in the Mediterranean and in central Europe, their commercial interests protected by alliance with the Carthaginians against the Greeks. The Greeks themselves had established a trading colony at Spina on the mouth of the Po, and many Greeks had emigrated into Etruria. In the 5th century, following the defeat at the Battle of Cumae in 474 BC, Etruscan power began to decline, her rule in Campania came to an end, and the Gauls began undermining her power in the north. In the 3rd century Etruria eventually succumbed to the rising power of Rome, and thereafter most of the famous Etruscan cities have no important part to play in history.

ROME AND ETRURIA

It is worthwhile stressing again that although Etruscan art is richly deserving of study for itself our main purpose in dealing with it in this book is to understand the background

51. **The 'High Priestess'.** Probably 5th century BC. Limestone. h. 4 ft. 5⅛ in. (1.35 m.). Archaeological Museum, Madrid. Iberian statue from the Cerro de Los Santos representing a priestess, or votary, wearing ceremonial dress and jewellery.

of Roman art. Rome, in the 6th century BC, was an Etruscan city ruled, according to tradition, by Etruscan kings, and what has survived of the architecture and sculpture of this period in the city, shows a complete dependence on the art of her Etruscan neighbours. When the Romans eventually overcame the Etruscans, most of the Etruscan cities were ruthlessly looted for works of art, especially bronze and stone sculptures, which went to adorn the public and private buildings of Rome. After the collapse of Etruria, it is hard to detect any basic change in the artistic tradition of central Italy until the 1st century BC. The same Etruscan techniques in architecture and the arts continued to be practised, although Rome was now the dominant power in central Italy. And so the Etruscan merges with the Roman.

THE 'VILLANOVANS'

The 'Villanovan' culture of Etruria in the 8th century is closely related to the other Iron Age cultures of Italy. The principal burial rite is cremation, the ashes of the dead being interred in a characteristic ossuary, the biconical urn (figure 52), which is covered either with a small cup or by a bronze helmet. The Villanovans were skilled bronze-workers, making and decorating bronze armour and *fibulae*, and domestic vessels; their pottery was wheel-made in a grey-black fabric known as *impasto*. In the 8th century both pottery and metalwork were decorated in a geometric style, with incised meanders, zigzags, lines and so on, which is obviously related to the geometric style in Greece, but lacks its precision and strong sense of order. The human figure does not appear at all in the earliest stage.

The Greeks established their first colony in southern Italy, at Cumae, about 750 BC and the Villanovan geometric style probably derives from imitation of Greek pottery, which was certainly being imported into Etruria at a very early period. By about 700 BC, or perhaps a little later, we find painted pottery being made in the Etruscan area, which provides us with the first clear-cut imitation of Greek work; a well-known vase from Bisenzio, in the Villa Giulia Museum, Rome, is decorated with geometric ornament and a narrow frieze of dancing figures in characteristic geometric silhouette. The earliest figure-sculpture, too, is closely inspired by Greek geometric art. Like Greek work, it is all on a small scale; animal figures serve as supports for metal vessels, or are attached to clay vases. There is, for example, a clay vase decorated in Villanovan style from Bologna, which has a bull's head spout and is surmounted by the figure of a little geometric horse with helmeted rider.

THE 'ORIENTALISING' PHASE

The 7th century sees the rapid development of prosperity in Etruria. Members of the Etruscan ruling class were buried in elaborate chamber tombs, and these tombs were richly furnished with pottery, bronzes and objects of precious metal. In a family burial, called the Regolini-Galassi tomb, at Caere, the dead were buried with magnificent

52. **Funerary Urn.** 7th century BC. Terracotta. h. 14¼ in. (36 cm.). British Museum, London. Biconical urn of Villanovan type decorated with incised geometric ornament.

jewellery, handsome vessels of gold and silver, objects of ivory and amber, and other luxury materials. In this period the wealth of Etruria attracted trade from all over the Mediterranean world. There were imports from Greece, Egypt, northern Syria and Phoenicia, and imitations of imported work in Greek and orientalising styles. The lavish gold jewellery (plates 85, 86), typical of the Etruscan taste of the time, is overloaded with ornamental detail, mostly of oriental inspiration. Much of it is carried out in the granulation technique — the use of tiny gold granules to make ornamental patterns — in which the Etruscans achieved a high degree of mastery. The gold cup from the Bernardini Tomb at Praeneste (plate 87) has a Greek shape; the un-Greek feature is the presence of little oriental sphinxes on top of the handles, a feature reminiscent of the famous Cup of Nestor from the Fourth Shaft Grave at Mycenae.

The first attempts at a monumental sculpture are found in the 7th century. There are some early stone sculptures from Vetulonia based on oriental models, and oriental influence shows very strongly in the face of the seated statuette of a woman from Caere, illustrated in plate 84. The 7th-century Canopic jars from Chiusi have heads whose primitive character is modified by Greek and oriental models. According to tradition, it was the Corinthians who first introduced to Etruria the arts of modelling in terracotta, at which the Etruscans were to excel, and it was a Greek, Aristonothos, who signed a painted vase of the later 7th century, found at Tarquinia. It is very likely that native Etruscan craftsmen were responsible for some of the products, especially those which show an obvious mingling

53. **Statuette of a Woman.** *c.* 600 BC.
Alabaster. h. 2 ft. 9½ in. (85 cm.). British
Museum, London. This statuette, found
in the Isis Tomb near Vulci in 1839,
is closely related in style to 7th-century
Greek sculpture.

of Villanovan and foreign elements, but there is little doubt
that the best work was done by foreigners. The result is that
the 7th century does not see the creation of a firm Etruscan
artistic tradition, comparable to that which developed in
Greece following its orientalising phase. Instead, at the
end of the 7th century, new Greek influences begin to assert
themselves in Etruria, and, from then on, successive waves
of Greek influence dictating the general development of
Etruscan art.

EARLY ETRUSCAN SCULPTURE

Let us look first at Etruscan sculpture. Etruria lacks the
rich resources of statuary marble that are readily available
in Greece, and the quarries of Carrara, which produce a
good marble, were not exploited until the 1st century BC.
The chief materials of sculpture were terracotta, bronze
and the local stones, including the alabaster of the Volterra
region. Terracotta was used both for making large statues,
and for protective facings and architectural decoration of
wooden temples and other buildings. Stone was used for
free-standing figures, sarcophagi and funerary urns. Bronze
was the principal material for statuary, but, as in the case
of Greece, comparatively little full-size bronzework has
survived. The Etruscans were also famous for high-class
bronze utensils, which made considerable use of small-scale
figures to decorate them; tripods, candelabra, bronze
vessels with figure-attachments were made at many
Etruscan centres.

The alabaster figure of a woman, illustrated in figure 53,
comes from the Isis Tomb at Vulci, and is now in the British
Museum. This half life-sized figure was made around 600
BC, and in style it is closely related to 'Daedalic' sculptures
in Greece, at the period when more rounded forms had
begun to replace the sharpness and angularity of the earlier
Daedalic style. It is difficult to say whether this is in fact the
work of a Greek or an Etruscan, and perhaps it does not
matter, because there is so little to distinguish it from
Greek work. The same is true of a stone statue of a centaur
from Vulci, another work of the same period, whose big
eyes, square face, narrow waist and broad shoulders, are
strongly reminiscent of the 7th-century Peloponnesian
'canon' for the human figure. What these sculptures lack is
the polish and refinement of the best Greek work.

Vulci, where both these figures were made, was the
leading sculptural centre in central Etruria; Veii and Caere
led in the south. In the 6th century the influence of the
Greek colonies of Campania, where Greek and Etruscan
lived side by side for over a hundred years, became very
strong in Etruria. Artists at Caere seem to have learnt from
Campania the art of revetting their wooden buildings with
terracotta plaques, and Campanian bronzework was
much prized in Etruria. During the 7th century, Corinthian painting and sculpture had dominated the art of
Etruria, but by the 6th century Corinthian influence was
being replaced by stronger influences from Ionian Greece,
and this can be seen particularly clearly in painting.

54. **Women revellers.** *c.* 500 BC.
Limestone. h. 1 ft. 6½ in. (47 cm.).
British Museum, London. This scene is
carved on a funerary stone *(cippus)* made
at Chiusi, in Etruria. These *cippi* held
cremation burials.

TERRACOTTA SCULPTURES FROM SOUTHERN ETRURIA

The school of terracotta sculpture that flourished in southern Etruria towards the end of the 6th century, has been associated with the name of Vulca of Veii, the famous Etruscan who was called in by the Romans to decorate the temple of Capitoline Jupiter. The school of Veii stands out from the mass of derivative Etruscan art. In the 6th century, the Etruscans had adopted the Greek archaic figure types, the *kouros* and *kore*, and had learnt the Greek conventions of drapery and the rendering of the human form. More important, they had adopted the Greek anthropomorphic conception of the gods, and conflated Greek divinities with their own. Yet nothing could be further from the Greek conception of Apollo than the figure from Veii (plate 93), which once formed part of a group apparently decorating the ridge of a temple roof. The subject of the group was the struggle between Apollo and Herakles, who has tried to steal the holy hind of the god. The god is shown advancing swiftly against his opponent, with his drapery clinging tightly to his body in a pattern of regular folds. The strength and power of the figure has nothing of the aloofness of the Greek ideal. The terracotta sarcophagus from Caere, now in the Villa Giulia Museum, with a man and his wife shown reclining on the lid, was made about the same period as the Apollo. Here the Etruscan sculptor has captured the tenderness of the scene by a subtle use of gesture and expression in the faces; he has devoted much more attention to the movements of the hands, and the look on the faces, than to the forms of the body. His approach seems fundamentally different from the contemporary Greek.

The differences between late archaic sculpture in Greece and Etruria come out well in a comparison of the Greek banqueter (plate 35) and the Etruscan satyr-banqueter (plate 92). In the one all is delicacy and refinement, with a strong sense of the bodily forms underlying the contours of the drapery; in the other the head is made more vividly expressive by exaggerating its scale, while the elongated body is lost below the rich patterning and flowing lines of the drapery.

FIFTH- AND FOURTH-CENTURY ETRUSCAN SCULPTURE

The development of the Greek ideal in the 5th century BC corresponds with the beginnings of decline in the fortunes of the Etruscans, and there is nothing corresponding to the process of artistic revolution that we observe in Greece. The Tyskiewicz head (figure 56), in the British Museum, made perhaps about 480–470 BC, shows how the archaic style lingers on into the 5th century and the head has a hardness that could never be mistaken for contemporary Greek work. It is not until late in the 5th century that we see some reflection of the 5th-century Greek achievement in the local sculpture of Etruria. A group of sculptors working on a temple at Orvieto (Via S. Leonardo), seem to have been inspired by late 5th-century Athenian sculpture. They aim at the same quiet dignity of expression and the same rich effects of drapery and strength of form. The well-known figure of Mars from Todi, an almost life-size

55. **Relief from Taranto.** 4th century
BC. Limestone. Taranto Museum. This
relief, from the decoration of a tomb at
Tarentum in southern Italy, probably
depicts an underworld scene.

56. **Head of a young man.** Early 5th
century BC. Bronze. h. 6 in. (15.5 cm.).
British Museum, London. The head is
a good example of late archaic Etruscan
work under Greek influence.

bronze made in the early 4th century, has something of the
grandeur and simplicity of a Greek divinity, but the head is
disproportionately large and the balance of the figure lacks
the Greek sense of symmetry. The bronze Chimaera from
Arezzo, which probably belongs to the same period, is one
of the finest examples of animal sculpture that has survived
from the ancient world.

HELLENISTIC SCULPTURE IN CENTRAL ITALY

The revival of Etruscan art in the 3rd century BC should
probably be looked upon as a revival of central Italian art
under the guidance of Rome. New Greek influences from
the southern Italian colonies now reached central Italy,
largely as a result of Roman expansion. But because the
traditional materials continued to be used together with
traditional techniques, this revived art still has the look of
being Etruscan, although Etruria had in fact ceased to be
a power. The sculptures from the Temple of Lo Scasato, at
Civ ità Castellana, were made about the middle of the 3rd
century BC. The magnificent head of Apollo, from the pediment of the temple, is modelled in a style related to the
work of Lysippus' pupils. A remarkable head from Arezzo
is very like the strangely intense Scopaic heads from the
Temple at Tegea (plate 60), with the same square contours
of the upthrust face and the 'pathetic' expression in the
deep-set eyes. It was probably made about 200 BC.

The realism of Hellenistic art, and the interest in portraiture, found a ready response in central Italy, where a
strong interest in the details of the individual face had been
apparent from the first. The head had stood for the man

57. **Ulysses and the Sirens.** 2nd century BC. Alabaster. h. 1 ft. 3⅜ in. (39 cm.). British Museum, London. This scene appears on an Etruscan funerary urn made in Volterra.

on the Canopic jars of Chiusi, and the practice of dedicating votive heads at tombs and sanctuaries seems to have gone on throughout the Etruscan period, a practice which must have had its influence on the Roman tradition of ancestral portraiture. A rich series of funerary sculptures, from sarcophagi to ash-urns (figures 57, 58), provides the principal source for the development of portraiture in central Italy, but there are also some fine bronze portrait heads and figures of the last two centuries BC. In the terracotta votive-heads the individual is portrayed with a down-to-earth simplicity, which is generally free of any idealisation. The bronze portrait head of a boy from Fiesole (plate 100), now in the Louvre, is a masterpiece of direct and vivid portraiture, of the kind which the Roman patricians of the last century BC demanded of the sculptors who worked for them. The most famous of all the late Etruscan portraits is the so-called *Arringatore*, the statue of an orator (plate 98), which bears an inscription in Etruscan, but portrays a Roman citizen, Aulus Metellus. It is the first of the long line of portrait statues of Romans, which form so important a part of Roman art throughout the Empire.

In late Etruscan relief-sculpture on buildings, sarcophagi and urns, we can follow both the developments in Hellenistic relief and the appearance of distinctively Italian themes. The subjects are taken mainly from Greek mythol-ogy and history, but local history and religious practices also appear. All the styles of later Greek relief-sculpture are reflected in the funerary reliefs, from the balanced action of battle scenes like the Amazon frieze on the Mausoleum at Halicarnassus, to the dynamic style of the massed compositions on the frieze of the Pergamene Altar. The heroic emotionalism of the latter seems to have appealed particularly to central Italian taste. A 2nd-century terracotta frieze from Città Alba represents the attack by the Gauls on Delphi in 279. It seems to provide a link between the Greek representations of history and the Roman idea of the historical frieze, since it treats of a specific event and introduces a good deal of precise detail, in contrast with the more generalised or completely allegorical commemoration of history that we find in Greece. Some of the Volterran urns show ritual scenes, in a straightforward factual style that has much in common with Roman commemorative art. A group of terracotta pedimental sculptures from Via S. Gregorio, Rome, reminds us that temples were still being built in Etruscan style at Rome during the last century BC. The subject is a sacrificial scene of the kind which became common in Imperial relief-sculpture.

ETRUSCAN TOMB-PAINTING

The almost complete loss of monumental painting in

58. **Sarcophagus of the Magnate.**
3rd century BC. h. 6 ft. 9½ in. (2.07 m.).
Tarquinia Museum. Etruscan stone
sarcophagus, with reclining figure of the
dead man on the lid. The reliefs depict a
battle between Greeks and Amazons.

Greece has been stressed in the earlier chapters of this book.
In Etruria, on the other hand, a rich legacy of large-scale
paintings inspired by Greek sources, decorate the walls of
chamber tombs at Tarquinia, and elsewhere. The paintings
are carried out on a layer of lime plaster in the fresco
technique; the earliest examples belong to the 6th century
BC, and the series extends right down to the 1st century BC.
The Etruscan idea, that the tomb is a place where the dead
live on, lies behind the subject-matter of the paintings.
Scenes in the earlier period are taken from daily life—banqueting, games, hunting and so on. In the later tombs,
underworld scenes peopled by frightening demons show
what seems to be a complete change in the Etruscan attitude to death; even the banquet scenes take on a melancholy air (plate 95).

THE EARLIEST PAINTING

Before the development of monumental painting in Etruria, the Etruscans were already imitating Greek painted
pottery. We have already mentioned some examples of the
geometric style, and in the 7th century the products of
Corinthian potters, which commanded the foreign markets
in the period, were copied in the so-called Italo-Corinthian
vases. During the 6th century, Ionian Greek influence
dominated the local painted pottery of Etruria. A group of

black-figured vases, the so-called Caeretan *hydriae* (water-
pots), seem to have been made about the middle of the 6th
century BC, by immigrant Ionian craftsmen in Caere. The
style is Ionian, the subjects lively and sometimes humorous
versions of Greek mythology (plate 90). The earliest monumental tomb-paintings belong to about the same period.
In the scene from the Tomb of the Bulls, one of the earliest
of the archaic painted tombs of Etruria (plate 88), Achilles
is waiting in a thicket behind a fountain to ambush the
Trojan prince Troilus. The inspiration comes from vase-
painting, but despite the Greek models there is much that
seems characteristically Etruscan, especially the introduction of trees and plants into the scene, the powerfully
dramatic rendering of the ambush, and the strange in-
congruities of scale. There is something, too, of the same
spirit of irony that we see in the Caeretan hydriae.

THE EARLY TOMBS OF TARQUINIA

In the archaic tombs of Tarquinia, the technique is outline
drawing with flat washes of colour—reds, greens, blues and
yellows. There are conventions of brown for the skin of the
men, and a paler wash for the women; trees and shrubs
appear as filling ornaments in the most unexpected con-
texts. Within the conventions of archaic art, the artists
paint with a liveliness that delights in exaggerated gesture

59. **Trojan Captives.** *c.* 300 BC. Bronze. h. 1 ft. 2½ in. (36.5 cm.). British Museum, London. Detail of the engraving on a bronze *cista* from Palestrina, showing the sacrifice of Trojan captives at the funeral of Patroclus.

and violent movement. Even though the essence of the style is Greek, the artists often seem to be indulging a taste for realistic detail, and an interest in nature which is wholly un-Greek. It is in the *Tomb of Hunting and Fishing* that the contrast between the Greek and Etruscan approach comes out best. Here are scenes which show a genuine delight in the world of nature; in the fishing scene the landscape is painted with loving care and the figures do not dominate the scene. 'Man is a feature of the landscape', says one critic. One is reminded strongly of the wall paintings of Knossos, where nature inspires the same colourful decorative art. But it would be wrong to contrast the lively colourful painting of Etruria with the monotonous black-and-red world of the Greeks that we see in their vase-painting. Etruscan paintings show the same palette that must have been used in the lost mural paintings of Greece, and may be taken as some evidence for it.

The archaic series of Etruscan tomb-paintings extends to about the middle of the 5th century BC. The most famous are those of the *Tomb of the Augurs*, the *Tomb of the Triclinium*, with perhaps the finest of the whole series, and the *Tomb of the Leopards* (plate 91). Etruscan painting shows little of the developments and experiments in foreshortening, and the rendering of the human figure that characterise late archaic art in Greece; there is hardly a trace of the Greek revolution of the early 5th century, and the paintings as late as the mid-5th century are still predominantly archaic.

LATER PAINTINGS

As in sculpture, so in painting there is a big gap between the archaic tombs and those of the 4th century, when Greek inspiration finds a new creative response in Etruria. When the series begins again, we see evidence for developments in representational art that have taken place in the intervening period. One of the finest examples of ancient painting that has come down to us may be seen on the painted sarcophagus from Tarquinia in Florence; one scene (plate 96), of a chariot driven by Amazons, is painted in a style which shows a mastery of chiaroscuro effects and a skilful handling of foreshortening. The painting is purely Greek in spirit, and one suspects that the artist was a Greek of southern Italy. The head of Arnth Velcha's wife, from the Tomba dell'Orco at Tarquinia (plate 97), is painted in a fine Greek style, with a subtle use of shading on the face. The hideous demons who people the underworld of later Etruscan painting, are utterly un-Greek in spirit. Greek art had rid itself of its legacy of monsters, but those of the Etruscans are painted with a morbid love of horrifying colour and detail. The banquet scenes of the later period introduce portraits of the dead, painted with close attention to facial likeness, especially in the men (plate 95). The François tomb from Vulci combines painted scenes, taken from Greek mythology, with scenes of local history. It seems to be one of the latest in the series of Etruscan tomb-paintings and by its choice of subjects brings us near to the tradition of Roman commemorative painting.

VASE-PAINTING AND DRAWING FROM THE FOURTH CENTURY

Local imitation of Greek vases went on throughout the Etruscan period, but it is not until the 4th century that we find in central Italy a style of vase-painting with really independent characteristics. The big red-figured vases produced in Falerii (Cività Castellana), in the 4th century, are painted in a lively and distinctive style. The scene on a big crater by the Nazzano painter, illustrated in plate 94, shows the sack of Troy; it is drawn in a rich style, vivid in detail and attractively different from the mass of southern Italian vase-painting of the same period. The compositional technique is still that of the 5th-century painters in Greece, though there is some suggestion of smaller scale for the more distant figures. The same representational method is used on some of the engraved bronze vessels produced, in a typically Etruscan technique, during the 4th century (see figure 59). The finest surviving example is the so-called *Ficoroni Cista*, in the Villa Giulia Museum, Rome, which is signed by a Latin artist who states that he made it in Rome; the scene is taken from the story of the Argonauts. The engraving shows a mastery of the principles of foreshortening, skilfully introduces landscape details into the scene, and makes the more distant figures smaller than those of the foreground. The figures on the handle and feet of this vessel are exquisite examples of Etruscan bronzework, but with just that slight harshness of detail, carelessness in proportions, oddity of pose, that distinguish Etruscan from Greek work of the same period.

ETRUSCAN ARCHITECTURE AND THE ROMANS

We cannot deal in detail with the architecture of the Etruscan area; our chief interest in Etruscan art comes from the fact that it provides the background to Roman art, and it is from that point of view that we shall treat briefly the history of Etruscan architecture. We know, in fact, very little about the principal Etruscan cities, and, in general, it is one of the main difficulties in understanding Etruscan culture that our sources of evidence come from funerary monuments. None of the famous Etruscan cities has been thoroughly excavated, and we can only generalise about the character of the buildings and layout. The Etruscan cities were built on easily defensible sites, and were not given elaborate circuits of defensive walls until a later period. It seems fairly clear that the cities grew up haphazardly from Villanovan beginnings, without the regular layout which was associated in later times with Etruscan town-planning. But the small Etruscan town of Marzabotto, founded near Bologna in the early 5th century, has a strictly formal plan, with principal streets crossed by narrower subsidiary streets, creating rectangular building plots such as we find in the regular layouts of later Greek and Roman town-plans. The streets were well paved and efficiently drained; the houses were of brick, stone and timber. The basic form of the Etruscan house was rectangular, consisting of a single room partitioned in various ways. The more elaborate plans are known to us from Etruscan tombs, which, as we have seen, often imitated the houses of the living. In these more ambitious plans, we see a form of house which is preserved in the domestic architecture of the Roman Empire; the main feature is a central chamber, the *atrium*, which has three rooms opening off it at one end, and is approached on the opposite side by a passage with flanking rooms. The Romans, indeed, specifically attributed to Etruria one form of atrium, the so-called *atrium tuscanicum*, in which the roof has a downward tilt in all directions towards a central opening. Some of the internal details of the Etruscan house are also known from tombs; ceiling joists, doors, windows and furniture are carved in stone in some of the richer tombs.

TEMPLE DESIGN AND DECORATION

Etruscan towns were dominated by the temples of the gods, and Etruscan temple-architecture provides us with the most important evidence for the influence of Etruria on Rome. As we have seen, the Etruscan temple was built predominantly of wood, with the wooden members protected by facings of terracotta slabs. It developed under Greek influence, but like all branches of Etruscan art retained its own essential characteristics and traditional materials. Unlike the Greek temple, it was not transformed from wooden origins into monumental stone forms. The Etruscan temple, unlike the Greek, was raised up on a high podium approached by steps at the front. The basic plan seems to have consisted of a single chamber, fronted by a row of wooden columns of wide span supporting the porch, but a number of variant and more elaborate plans are found. Vitruvius specifically attributes to Etruscan invention the triple division of the main chamber of the temple, which later becomes characteristic of Roman temples dedicated to Jupiter, Juno and Minerva, the deities of the Capitoline Triad. The arrangement of the temple columns varied; there was never, so far as we know, a complete peristyle or colonnade all round the *cella*, but the columns might run along the sides, or there might be a double row along the front. Many of these details continued into the architecture of the Empire. The Roman temple always has a high podium, and the columns are generally related to the Etruscan arrangement rather than the Greek. It was surely the Etruscan taste for richness of detail in the brightly painted terracotta facings, that lay behind the Roman taste for elaborately carved ornamental detail on the buildings of the Empire. Apart from the terracotta facings, the structural elements of Etruscan temples are derived from Greek architecture. The typical Etruscan column is a simplified form of Doric with a plain shaft and a torus base. The pure Doric also makes its appearance, but without any of the refinement of detail that we find in Greek work. The 'Aeolic' capital, prototype, it seems, of the Greek Ionic, is also found in Etruria, and from the 4th century onwards, under the influence of south Italian art, Ionic and Corinthian come in together with various special forms of capital, such as capitals with figures and busts as decoration, but these elements are part of a general central Italian Hellenistic tradition, rather than a pure Etruscan one. The 'Tuscan Order' of Vitruvius seems to be a Roman 'rationalisation' of various Etruscan elements.

BUILDING METHODS

Etruscan methods of building are basically similar to those of the Greeks. Polygonal and ashlar wall building is found in the Etruscan cities, none of which seem to have been walled before about 400 BC. The early tombs are often vaulted in a technique similar to that used for the Mycenaean chamber tombs, where overlapping horizontal courses are used to cover passages and domed structures. There has been much discussion about the origins of the true arch and vault, and the invention has been attributed to the Etruscans. In fact, it is very difficult to make a special claim for its origin in Etruria, but it does seem that the development of the arch as a vital architectural form took place in Italy in the last centuries BC. By about 100 BC, in central Italy, we find it used in conjunction with engaged columns and pilasters, for example, in the city-gates of the Etruscan city of Perugia; but this use belongs to the period of 'Italic-Hellenistic' architecture in Italy, which is not a pure Etruscan tradition. At this time the arch was already being used in a similar way in the eastern Greek world, though it had not perhaps achieved the same popularity.

By about 80 BC, as we shall see, the big monuments of Rome and Latium were making use of the arch, and of the concrete vault, in conjunction with the Greek orders of architecture, in a way which leads on directly to the great achievements of Roman Imperial building. Although we cannot attribute the invention of the arch and vault to Etruria, we can claim that it found popularity in the Etruscan area, because of the deficiencies of the local supplies of fine building stone, and because one of the main characteristics of Etruscan art in general was its enthusiastic acceptance of new ideas from Greece.

ROME AND ETRURIA AGAIN

At the beginning of this chapter, we stressed that our main interest in the art of the Etruscans was as an essential element in the development of the Roman tradition. The danger is of underestimating, rather than overestimating, the Etruscan contribution. Everyone can recognise in the developed Roman temple elements which are certainly derived from Etruria, but it is perhaps not so readily understood that the Etruscan tradition of Hellenised art lies behind Rome's enthusiastic acceptance of Greek art in the 1st century BC, which we shall discuss in the last chapter. The Romans had already become acquainted with Greek themes and methods of representation, long before their foreign contacts brought them direct knowledge of the Greek world, and it was through Etruria that they made their acquaintance. It is clear, too, that much of the independent character of Roman art has its origins in the Etrusco-Italic tradition—the enthusiasm for realistic portraiture, especially for the portrait-bust, the love of rich decoration, the delight in the world of nature. Like the Etruscans, the Romans never understood the aims and ideals of Greek art, but they used its achievements to their own purposes in very much the same way.

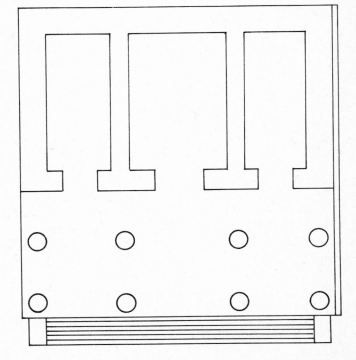

J. Plan of an Etruscan temple.

The Roman Empire

This chapter is concerned with Rome and her empire, the last phase of the classical world. From a small city-state community, for long under the power of the Etruscans, Rome had, by the end of the 3rd century BC, achieved domination of the whole of Italy, and laid the foundations of an empire abroad. In the 2nd century, Rome's influence began to assert itself over the whole Hellenistic world, and by the end of the 1st century all the Hellenistic kingdoms had succumbed to her power. She had also acquired rich possessions in the west; Spain had fallen to her after the Second Punic War, Gaul had been conquered by Caesar, parts of North Africa were under her control, even Britain had seen Roman troops in Caesar's two invasions. Under her old city-state form of government, Rome's foreign possessions were amateurishly, and often inefficiently, organised. The need for stronger rule was expressed in the struggle between the leading statesmen during the last century of the Roman Republic, which continued until in 31 BC when Caesar's heir, Octavian, defeated Mark Antony at the Battle of Actium, and established the Roman Empire.

THE ROMAN TASTE FOR GREEK ART

The Roman contribution to the history of art lies in the new stimulus given to the continuation of the Greek tradition, and the spread of a 'Greco-Roman' art over the whole area of the Roman Empire. To understand the art of the Roman age, we must first understand how the marriage of Roman imperialism and Greek artistic traditions came about. But it would be wrong to ignore the independent characteristics of Roman art, and the very great influence that those independent characteristics have had upon the subsequent development of art in Europe.

By the 3rd century BC, Rome had become the dominant power in central Italy, and was coming increasingly into contact with the Greek cities of southern Italy and of Greece itself. The triumphs of Roman generals in the 2nd century and later, were adorned with vast booty of works of art—sculpture, paintings, gold and silver—taken from conquered cities. The Etruscan background of Roman art, and the work of Greek artists from southern Italy, had created a sympathy and understanding for Greek art, which developed into a positive mania for collecting Greek art treasures. The acquisition of Pergamon in 133 BC, brought to Italy the hoarded wealth of the Attalid kings whose tastes in many ways coincided with those of the new world conquerors. The demand for Greek works of art among the Roman upper classes of the last century BC, was enormous; it was met by an influx of artists from all over the Hellenistic world, and also by the revival of artistic schools in many of the Greek cities. The bulk of their output was concerned with copying and adapting earlier work to decorate the interiors of houses with statuary, furniture and painting. The versatile school of Pasiteles in southern Italy, and that of the neo-Attics in Athens, which satisfied this aspect of Roman taste, have already been mentioned. But towards the end of the Republic, Greek artists were also commissioned to produce work for their Roman patrons, which was inspired by Roman traditions, and it is this work which is of far greater significance for the future history of art. Roman patricians wanted portraits of themselves and their ancestors, buildings and sculpture to commemorate historical events, and paintings to adorn their temples, and it was natural that they should turn to the superior skill of Greek artists and craftsmen to satisfy these demands.

THE TRADITIONS OF THE ROMAN REPUBLIC

The complex character of the art of the Roman Republic is best illustrated in the study of its portraiture. Rome had her own traditions of portraiture, among them that of preserving the likenesses of ancestors in the form of wax and clay masks, which were kept in the *atria* of their houses, and used on the occasion of family funerals. In some way connected with this custom was the practice of taking death-masks, and this practice must explain the presence of death-features in some of the funerary portraits of the last century BC (figure 61). Rome had also inherited the Etruscan tradition of commemorative portraiture—a tradition of strongly individualised likenesses, based on careful study of the features of the model, and not lacking the ability to express character. In the last century BC the final element in the creation of the Roman tradition of portraiture, the technical skill of Greek sculptors, was added; the portraits of the last great men of the Republic, of Caesar, Pompey, and the rest, show us this blend of Roman taste and Greek ability. Hellenistic influence gave more than refinement and the ability to give the features the stamp of fine portraiture. The Roman patricians also inherited some of the ideals of Hellenistic court-portraiture. Throughout the Empire the ideal of physical beauty expressed in the nude portrait figure, and the ideal of military prowess in the cuirassed warrior, run side by side with the traditional representation of the Roman citizen in the toga of domestic life.

THE ROMAN COMMEMORATIVE RELIEF

The origins of the Roman tradition of commemorative relief sculpture also go back to the last centuries of the Republic. Here again, the tradition is compounded of Roman, Italic and Greek elements. There seems to have been a fairly old tradition in Rome of commemorating historical events in painting, and we get some evidence for it in late Etruscan tomb-paintings, engravings and funerary reliefs. There is also one surviving fragment of a tomb-painting, showing scenes from a military campaign, which perhaps belongs to the tradition of commemorative paintings exhibited on the occasion of military triumphs; it was found in a tomb on the Esquiline Hill, in Rome, and probably dates from the 1st century BC. On the coinage of the last century BC, the reverse types show an interest in the direct commemoration of historical and political events. The earliest example of historical relief-sculpture inspired by an event of Roman history, is the frieze from the monument

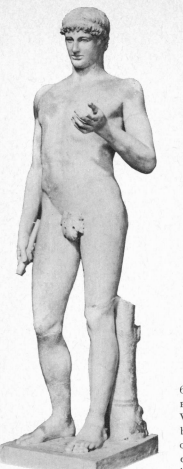

60. **Stephanos. An Athlete.** 1st century BC. Marble. h. 4 ft. 7⅛ in. (1.40 m.). Villa Albani, Rome. This statue is signed by Stephanos, who belonged to the school of Pasiteles. The style is eclectic, combining elements of a number of different periods in the history of Greek art.

61. **Tombstone of Gaius Septumius.** 1st century BC. h. 20½ in. (57 cm.). Ny Carlsberg Glyptotek, Copenhagen. The portrait of the dead man is one of a number of Roman portraits of the period which seem to show the influence of death masks.

put up by the general, Aemilius Paullus, in 168 BC, to commemorate his victory at the Battle of Pydna (figure 62). The sculptor was certainly a Greek, and his work is in many ways a typical Hellenistic battle scene. It is interesting, however, that a specific moment of significance in the battle, the episode of the runaway horse, has been chosen as the subject of the scene. There is an inkling here of the Roman liking for direct, straightforward representation of historical events, which is a leading characteristic of the finest achievements of Roman historical relief. In the last century BC, particularly towards its end, we find events of Roman history represented in a direct factual style by highly skilled Greek sculptors brought to Rome to work on the monuments of the capital.

REPUBLICAN ARCHITECTURE

In architecture, as in relief-sculpture and portraiture, the late Republic was the formative period of the specifically Roman tradition. The erection of buildings, in the traditional central Italian materials, continued right down to the time of the Empire, but in the last century new methods of construction and the use of new materials, were rapidly developed. There are a number of buildings in Rome and Latium, put up in the first half of the last century BC, which seem to show all the developed characteristics of Roman architecture in embryo. The most impressive is the Sanctuary of Fortuna Primigenia, at Palestrina, a vast complex

of buildings built in the form of a series of terraces against the natural slope of a hill and supported by means of concrete vaults and arches (figure K). Combined with the use of concrete construction is a decorative, and partly structural, use of classical columnar architecture. Pilasters and half-columns may serve to decorate the spaces between arches; columns give support to one side of a concrete vaulted passage. By the middle of the 1st century BC, Roman architects were using the same methods to build the permanent theatres that were to become so characteristic a part of Roman architecture. The combination of concrete vault construction, and the decorative use of the Greek orders, gave rise to an entirely new kind of building. Whereas the Greek theatre had made use of a natural slope to create the auditorium, and conceived the stage-building as a separate structure, the Romans were able to raise the auditorium from level ground on radial vaulting, and to integrate its design with that of the stage. The Greek inspiration for the general form of the Roman theatre is clear enough, but the differences are great (plate 115).

Differences are no less apparent in other kinds of building. In Rome during the last century BC, there were a few temples built in pure Greek form and style, generally by Greek architects, but the typical late Republican temple is a mixture of Etruscan, Italic, and Greek elements. One of the best examples is the little 'Temple of Fortuna Virilis', by the Tiber in Rome, put up in the last years of the Re-

62. **The Battle of Pydna.** 2nd century BC. Marble. Delphi Museum. Part of the sculptured frieze from a pillar erected at Delphi to commemorate the battle of Pydna (168 BC), at which L. Aemilius Paullus defeated Perseus, king of Macedon.

K. Reconstruction of the central part of the Sanctuary of Fortuna Primigenia at Praeneste (Palestrina).

public. Like the traditional Etruscan temple it stands on a high base or podium which is approached only by steps at the front. The architectural detail is a fairly pure version of Greek Ionic, but unlike a Greek temple the columns do not run all round the main chamber of the temple, but continue in the form of half-columns against the sides and back of the chamber. Here again we see a reflection of the typically Etruscan plan, with columns only at the front, and the whole design illustrates that mixture of conservatism and new ideas which characterises the art of the period. These essential forms were to survive right through the period of the Empire (see plate 103).

The purity of the classical tradition in ornament is completely alien to the taste of Roman architects. At Palestrina,

the forms of the Ionic and Corinthian capitals are not those of the eastern Hellenistic world where, to some extent, the purity of the Greek orders was still admired, especially by the more academic architects; the Romans used instead local versions inspired by southern Italian models. In the course of the 1st century BC, new and direct influence from the Hellenistic world led to the general adoption of more orthodox forms of the orders, but the essentially non-Greek background of Roman architecture was always likely to inspire a frivolous disregard for purity, and a liking for over-elaboration of ornamental detail. The Corinthian order was adopted as the Roman order par excellence because of its richer decorative possibilities, and combinations of the orders, which seem to have appealed especially to the

L. The Roman Corinthian Order.

M. Roman composite capital.

N. Reconstruction of the *Ara Pacis*, Rome.

Roman taste, led to the creation of the composite capital, a mixture of Ionic and Corinthian. The severe Doric order was almost completely rejected for large scale building. As in constructional method and design, so in ornament, the Roman taste differs very greatly from the Greek.

THE FOUNDATION OF THE EMPIRE

The foundation of the Roman Empire by Augustus did not fundamentally change the character of Roman art, but it completely altered the character of artistic patronage. The Roman State now became the chief patron of the arts, and the best talents were organised to work on an inspired propaganda programme, devised by Augustus and his circle of advisers. The building of new towns throughout Italy, and the provinces, gave a new stimulus to architecture and the arts. The Roman government continued to employ Greek artists and craftsmen to achieve their purposes, but their work was given a specifically Roman character by Roman aims and ideals. It is an age of anonymity in the arts; the artist declined to the level of the craftsman, whose work was admired for its skill. We know the names of very few painters and sculptors, and almost all of them are Greeks; their work satisfied every aspect of Roman taste—for grand buildings and commemorative monuments, for portraiture, for copies of Greek masterpieces, for decorative sculpture and painting, and it kept the classical tradition alive throughout the Empire. Only towards the end of the Empire, from the early 3rd century AD onwards, do we see evidence of tendencies in art which are opposed to classical ideals. They are the product of many different conditions of the time—the general decline of the Empire, the changes in religious beliefs, and many others—and, in many ways, they lead us on to a fundamentally different conception of the purpose and character of art in Byzantine and medieval times.

THE ARA PACIS IN ROME

The first great sculptured monument of the Imperial Age, is the *Ara Pacis*, in Rome, a monumental altar contained in a richly decorated rectangular enclosure, put up between 13 and 9 BC to commemorate the establishment of peace in the Roman world. The best available craftsmanship worked on its sculpture; there are exquisite arabesques of floral ornament in low relief carved in fine Hellenistic style, figured panels with allegorical compositions and scenes from Roman mythology, garlands of fruit and flowers, and a processional frieze commemorating the act of dedication of the altar in 13 BC. The whole decoration is a superb illustration of the way in which Greek talent was put to the service of imperial ideas; the processional frieze (figure 64) deserves our closest attention, for in it we see Greek and Roman ideas in the most harmonious combination. There is something of the Athenian ideal in the severe, noble conception of Roman citizenship contained in the figures, and the clarity of the 'Neo-Attic' style reminds us of the Parthenon frieze, but here the principal figures are not the ideal citi-

63. **Cup from Hoby.** Augustan period. Silver. h. 4¼ in. (10.9 cm.). Danish National Museum, Copenhagen. This scene on one of a pair of silver cups found in a rich man's grave at Hoby on the island of Laaland shows Priam appealing to Achilles for the return of Hector's body.

64. **A Roman procession.** *c.* 9 BC. Marble. h. 5 ft. 2 in. (1.57 m.). Part of the frieze from the *Ara Pacis* (Altar of Peace) in Rome, showing members of the Imperial family and officials in procession. The altar was built between 13 and 9 BC to commemorate Augustus' return from the western provinces of the Empire.

zens of 5th-century Greece, but portraits of distinguished Romans of the day. Their presence gives to the frieze the sense of a real event, of a moment of history.

THE DEVELOPMENT OF HISTORICAL RELIEF

The *Ara Pacis* laid the foundations of Imperial commemorative and decorative relief-sculpture, and the commemoration of historical events gives us some of the finest, and most typically Roman, achievements in sculpture. The two sculptured panels from the passage-way of the Arch of Titus are among the most famous; one of these shows us part of the triumphal procession of Vespasian and Titus, with the loot from the Temple of Jerusalem, brought to Rome after the Jewish War; in the other we see Titus, drawn in his chariot, and crowned by Victory. The processional panel (figure 65) makes a most subtle use of the different planes of relief to give an effective rendering of mass and movement, a development which takes us beyond the later achievements of Greek relief-sculpture into something which we may think of as specifically Roman. The strength of the Greek tradition is nowhere better seen than in the companion panel, where the allegorical figures, symbolising the various elements of the Roman people, are conceived in the tradition of Greek art. Indeed, throughout the early Empire we can see the Roman desire for factual, straightforward representation of events competing with an allegorical manner largely inspired by Greek models. In the magnificent spiral frieze on Trajan's column (figure 66), which depicts the Dacian campaigns of the Emperor, the factual style, with a wealth of accurate detail, prevails; in the time of Hadrian and the early Antonines the grand allegorical manner tends to assert itself in a rather pompous and overconfident expression of imperial ideas, which does much to inspire the strong reaction to classicism that we shall discuss in a later part of this chapter.

PORTRAITURE AND PROPAGANDA

The portraiture of the Emperor was one of the most important vehicles of imperial propaganda. The generals of the late Republic had already followed Hellenistic practice, and put their portraits on their coins, and they had gone to Greek artists to have busts and statues made of themselves. The creation of a satisfactory public image for the Emperor was a complex and subtle problem. Augustus' artistic advisers provided him with brilliant solutions. They preserved for us the features of the Emperor, but they treated them with an almost classical purity of style, that could give his lean ascetic countenance an almost divine majesty (plate 102). He could be all things to all men; now the devout, dedicated toga-clad Roman citizen, a great man among his fellows, now the forbidding symbol of imperial power that he presents in the famous statue from Prima Porta, in the Vatican (figure 67) where he stands clad in military costume, and in classical pose, making a simple but immensely expressive gesture of authority. Not all Emperors submit to these ideals in their portraits. Vespasian, proud of the

65. The Spoils of Jerusalem. *c.* AD 80.
Marble. The Arch of Titus, Rome. The
relief from the passage of the arch shows
part of the triumphal procession of Titus
in AD 71, after the conquest of Judea.
The booty from the Temple of Jerusalem
includes the table of shew-bread, trumpets
and seven-branched candle stick.

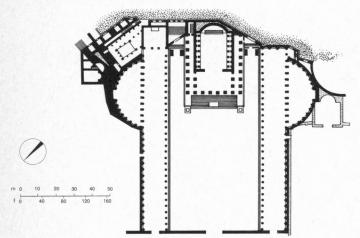

O. Plan of the Forum of Augustus, Rome.

66. Trajan's Column, Rome. *c.* AD 113.
Detail of the reliefs of the spiral frieze
on the marble column set up in Trajan's
Forum to commemorate the Emperor's
victories over the Dacians. The column
is 38 metres high, including its base and
column, and the frieze is over 50 metres
long.

simple Italic stock from which he had sprung, favours a
down-to-earth likeness, that reminds one of the portraiture
of Romans of the time of the Republic (figure 68), and in
the hands of the best artists conveys a power of personality
and a strength of purpose. One cannot imagine Vespasian
submitting to so comic a piece of portraiture as the statue
of Claudius as the god Jupiter, or anyone wishing to
portray him so (figure 69). Trajan, 'best of Emperors',
projects, in the portraits that have come down to us (figure
70), a wonderful image of benevolent rule, and the bearded
Hadrian, lover of things Greek, emerges almost as a Greek
hero (figure 76). The portraits of his favourite, Antinous,
combine the classical purity of his features and the ideals of
Greek sculpture in his body, making him a divinity almost
on the level of the great creations of the past (figure 75).
The Antonine emperors suffer from the technical preoccu-
pations of the sculptors of the time, who love the striking
effects of contrast between the high finish on the features
and the deeply drilled unruly mass of hair, but some of the
portraits of private individuals of this time are among the
finest studies of character that are preserved from the
Roman period (plate 118).

THE ACHIEVEMENTS OF ROMAN ARCHITECTURE

Architecture takes its full place in the propaganda programme of the Roman Empire. The rebuilding of Rome as
a worthy capital of a world Empire had been begun by
Julius Caesar, and his policy was extended by his successor,
Augustus, who boasted that he had found the city of Rome
built of brick and left it of marble. Buildings on the Roman
pattern were erected everywhere in the Empire—*fora* and
basilicas, triumphal arches, theatres and amphitheatres,
temples and sanctuaries. As we have seen, the basic forms
of most of these buildings had been created in the late Republic, but they now rose with a new magnificence, making
lavish use of plain and coloured marbles. Complexes of
buildings were planned on a grand scale, and the development of brick-faced concrete as a building technique in the
early Empire gave Roman buildings a completely different
character. Plate 112 gives a view of the Forum of Augustus,
in Rome, which was built by the emperor to extend the
administrative area of the city, and to be a monument of
imperial prestige. The Forum consists of an open area
flanked on two sides by colonnades and semicircular ex-
edras, and dominated by the massive temple of Mars Ultor
at one end. The design of the temple and the whole forum
area are characteristically Roman, but the architectural
detail is very largely Greek in spirit. The influence of 5th-
century Athens is particularly strong, and may be seen in
the copies of the Caryatids from the porch of the Erechtheum, at Athens, which served to decorate the upper order
of the flanking colonnades, and in the carved ornament on

(Continued on page 153)

98. **The Arringatore.** 2nd or 1st century
BC. Bronze. h. 5 ft. 11 in. (1.80 m.).
Archaeological Museum, Florence. This
famous statue was found at Sanguineto,
near Lake Trasimene. An inscription gives
the name of the man as Aule Metele, an
Etruscan version of the Roman name
Aulus Metellus. He is represented as an
orator making a grand gesture with his
right arm to emphasise a point. The figure
is one of the most striking ancient portrait
statues that has come down to us.

99. (above). **Portrait of a bearded man.**
c. 2nd century BC. Bronze. h. 12⅝ in.
(32 cm.). Conservatori Museum, Rome.
This head has been identified, but without
good reason, as L. Junius Brutus, the
founder of the Roman Republic. The
hard structure of the head and the flat
treatment of beard and hair suggest that
it belongs to the late Etruscan tradition
of portraiture. The eyes were inlaid with
enamel, brown for the iris and white
for the eyeballs.

100. (above). **Head of a young man
from Fiesole.** Bronze. h. 11⅝ in.
(29.6 cm.). Louvre, Paris. Head of a
young man, found in the environs of
Fiesole, not far from Florence. This portrait of a fleshy-faced youth is a lively
piece in the late Etruscan tradition of
portrait sculpture, with a fine momentary
expression and a clear individual
characterisation.

101. (right). **Head of a Roman of the
early Empire.** Bronze. Palazzo Barberini,
Rome. The figure, from which this detail
is taken, holds in his hands two busts of
his ancestors, probably those of his father
and grandfather. Though carved in the
Augustan period, the portrait still shows
something of the hard, dry style of the
late Republic.

102. (right). The Emperor Augustus.
1st century AD. Sardonyx. h. 5 in.
(12.8 cm.). British Museum, London.
The Emperor wears an *aegis* and *gorgo-neion*, symbols of his invincible power.
The diadem of gold and gems is a medi-eval addition to the cameo. This is one of
a series of fine cameo portraits of members
of the Roman imperial house and has been
attributed to Dioscorides, who was court
gem-engraver to the emperor.

**103. (below). The Maison Carrée at
Nîmes.** Early 1st century AD. The Maison
Carrée at Nîmes (Nemausus), in Provence,
is one of the most famous and best-preserved temples of the Roman Empire.
Like most Roman temples it stands on a
high base (*podium*), with access to the
temple chamber by means of steps at the
front. The columns do not form a peristyle
all round the chamber, but are continued
as half-columns engaged against the
chamber wall, a scheme which is known
as 'pseudo-peripteral'. The temple was
built during the reign of the Emperor
Augustus.

104. (below). **The Ephesian Artemis.**
1st century AD. Alabaster and bronze.
h. 6 ft. 8 in. (2.03 m.). National Museum,
Naples. The cult statue of the goddess
Artemis, 'Diana of the Ephesians', multi-
breasted, wearing a turretted crown, and
with the lower part of her body richly
decorated with symbolic reliefs, is one of
the strangest figures that has come down
to us from classical antiquity. This Roman
copy illustrates the Roman taste for poly-
chromy in statuary and architecture.

105. (above). **Kritios of Athens.
Mithras slaying the bull.** *c.* 2nd century
AD. Marble. h. 5 ft. 7 in. (1.70 m.). Ostia
Museum, Rome. The central event of
Mithraic mythology was represented
either in relief or in the round in all
Mithraic shrines. This group was found
in the underground Mithraeum in the
Baths of Mithras at Ostia, the port of
Rome. It is unusual in that it does not
represent the god as he usually appears
in Persian dress, but in Greek dress.
It is the work of an Athenian sculptor.

106. (left). **Polychrome Jug.** 3rd century BC. Glass. h. 5½ in. (14 cm.). British Museum, London. A multi-coloured vessel made by a process of winding strips of glass in a viscous state over a sand core. Moulded glass was also made in Hellenistic times, and glass-blowing, invented towards the end of the Hellenistic period, was practised throughout the Roman period.

107. (right). **Statuette of a girl.** 1st century AD. Bronze. h. 6 in. (15 cm.). British Museum, London. This small figure of a girl is said to come from Verona. The style imitates, but not consistently, archaic sculpture in Greece; such archaising works were very popular in Italy in the 1st century BC and the 1st century AD.

108. (below). **Wall painting from the Villa of Livia.** Early 1st century AD. h. 6 ft. 6¾ in. (2 m.). Museo Nazionale delle Terme, Rome. Livia was the wife of the Emperor Augustus, whom she outlived; the Emperor Tiberius was her son by a previous marriage. Garden scenes like this one taken from her villa at Prima Porta, near Rome, were very popular in the interior decoration of Roman houses during the early Empire.

109. (above). **The Trojan Horse.** 1st
century AD. h. 1 ft. 4 in. (39 cm.). Fresco.
National Museum, Naples. In the foreground of this picture the horse is being
dragged into the city by a group of men.
They are caught in a ghostly glow of light.
The towers and walls of the city can be
seen dimly in the background. The clever
effects of light, painted in a rapid impressionistic technique, give an eerie atmosphere to the scene and a powerful sense
of drama. From a house at Pompeii.

110. (below, left). **Theseus triumphant.**
1st century AD. Fresco. h. 3 ft. (92 cm.).
National Museum, Naples. In this picture,
from the wall of a house at Pompeii,
Theseus, who has slain the Minotaur, is
greeted by the Athenian children, whose
lives he has saved. On the right are a
group of spectators. A number of similar
versions of this subject have been found
at Pompeii, and they were probably
inspired by a famous Greek picture.
The original was probably painted in
the 4th or 3rd century BC.

111. (below, right). **Perseus rescuing
Andromeda.** 1st century AD. Fresco.
h. 4 ft. (122 cm.). National Museum,
Naples. There are a number of versions
of this subject among the wall paintings
from Pompeii, and it seems likely that the
inspiration comes from a famous picture
of the 4th century BC or the Hellenistic
period. The painting shows considerable
skill in modelling with colour, and in the
handling of light and shade.

112. (above). **The Forum of Augustus.**
Completed 2 BC. This view from the south
shows the massive back-wall of the Forum,
and the base and three standing columns
of the Temple of Mars Ultor, which was
the principal building. In front of the
temple was an open space flanked by
colonnades built in two storeys; the upper
storey was adorned with figures of
Caryatids copied from the Erechtheum
at Athens. The series of imperial *fora*
was built by the Emperors to extend the
administrative centre of the capital.

113. (above, right). **The Colosseum,
Rome.** AD 70–80. The great amphitheatre
built under the Flavian Emperors on the
site of the lake of Nero's Golden House in
Rome. The massive elliptical building
served for gladiatorial shows and other
spectacles; it is estimated to have held
45,000 people. The building is the finest
example of the skill of Roman architects
in supporting a massive auditorium on
arches and vaults. The classical orders of
architecture are used to decorate the
exterior of the building.

114. (below, right). **Wall painting from
the House of the Vettii, Pompeii.**
c. AD 70. Fresco. The wall is decorated in
what is called the 'Fourth Style' of Pompeian wall-painting, combining blank
areas of wall, on which are painted
imitation panel pictures, with views into
distant architecture. This scheme belongs
to the later years of Pompeii, not long
before its destruction in AD 79.

115. (far right). **The Theatre at Orange.**
1st century AD. The interior of the Roman
theatre at Orange (Arausio), in Provence,
one of the best preserved theatres in the
Roman Empire. The massive back wall
of the stage, which is a characteristic
feature of Roman theatres, has turret-like
projections, and was originally decorated
with elaborate marble architecture. The
external wall of this stage building was
described by Louis XIV as 'the finest
wall in my kingdom'.

116. (above). **The aqueduct at Nîmes.**
1st century AD. l. 885 ft. (270 m.), h. 160 ft.
(49 m.). The 'Pont du Gard', an aqueduct
carrying water from Uzès to Nîmes in
Provence, is one of the finest surviving
examples of the magnificent engineering
works carried out everywhere in the
Roman Empire. It has three storeys of
arches, six at the bottom, ten in the
middle, and a series of smaller arches in
the top storey carrying the actual conduit.

117. (below). **The Forum Romanum.**
A view of the central area of the Roman
Forum from the west, looking towards the
Temple of Antoninus and Faustina,
which was converted into a Christian
church in medieval times. The three
columns on the right of the picture belong
to the temple of Castor and Pollux. The
Basilica of Constantine and the Colosseum
can be seen in the distance.

118. (above). **Bust of a Roman citizen.**
c. AD 160. Bronze. h. 7½ in. (19 cm.).
British Museum, London. Hollow cast,
the eyes are inlaid with silver and garnets.
The head was made about AD 160.

119. **Equestrian statue of Marcus Aurelius.** AD 161–180. Bronze. h. 16 ft. 8 in. (5.08 m.). Rome. This statue of the Emperor now stands in the Piazza del Campidoglio, at Rome. It may once have stood above a triumphal arch erected to commemorate the Emperor's victories. In the Middle Ages the statue, which is the finest imperial bronze group surviving, was taken to represent Constantine the Great, a fact to which it owes its preservation. It was put in its present position by Michelangelo in 1538.

120. (left). **Bodhisattva of the Ghandara School, India.** 1st or 2nd century AD. Bronze. h. 3 ft. (91 cm.). British Museum, London. Ghandara sculpture seems to show strong influence from the Greco-Roman world, which may be recognised here in the treatment of the hair and drapery, especially the lower folds.

121. (above). **Bust of a woman from Palmyra.** 2nd century AD. Marble. h. 1 ft. 7½ in. (49.5 cm.). British Museum, London. Palmyrene funerary sculpture illustrates the mingling of Greco-Roman and oriental elements in the art of frontier lands of the Empire.

122. (right). **Roman mummy-portrait of a man.** 2nd century AD. h. 1 ft. 4 in. (40.6 cm.). British Museum, London. (Reproduced by courtesy of the Trustees of the National Gallery, London). This portrait, painted in coloured wax on wood, was found at Hawara in Egypt. Portraits of this kind were inserted into the wrappings of mummies from the 1st to the 4th century AD, and include some of the finest examples of painted portraiture that have survived from the ancient world.

123. (above). **The entrance to Diocletian's palace at Split.** *c.* AD 300. The Emperor Diocletian built this palace near Salona in Dalmatia for his retirement. It is protected by strong towered walls, and laid out like a military camp. The porch giving access to the palace proper consists of four massive granite columns with an architrave that breaks out into an arch over the two centre columns. Above is a pediment. The porch stands at the end of the main colonnaded street.

124. (below). **The Baths of Caracalla, Rome.** AD 211–217. Part of the *frigidarium* of the Baths. The arch on the left gave access to the great hall, which was the principal room of the bath building and was roofed by a series of three concrete cross-vaults supported upon huge piers. Massive columns of granite stood against the piers and the whole brick and concrete structure was given a rich veneer of classical architecture. The baths remained in operation until the 6th century AD, when the Roman aqueducts were finally broken down.

125. (above). **The Tetrarchs of St. Mark's, Venice.** *c.* AD 284–305. Porphyry. 4 ft. 6 in. (1.30 m.). These two pairs of imperial portraits now stand at the south-west corner of the Treasury of St. Mark's, Venice. The portraits are of Diocletian and his colleagues in the tetrarchy, Maximianus Herculius, Constantius I and Galerius, wearing military dress. The figures were brought from Palestine during the Middle Ages.

126. The Basilica of Constantine, Rome. This building was begun by Maxentius between AD 306 and 310 and completed by Constantine. It is one of the most impressive examples of late Roman architecture. The basilica stands by the *Via Sacra* in Rome, and was modelled on the great halls of Roman bath buildings. The main entrance was at the east, and at the west end there was an apse, originally intended for a tribunal, but later used for a colossal seated figure of Constantine, fragments of which still survive. This view looks westwards along the northern side-aisle, the best preserved part of the building.

127. (above). **Nereïds and Sea-Monsters.** Late 3rd century AD. Mosaic. This theme, of sea-maidens and sea-monsters was one of the most popular in the repertory of Roman decorative art. These rich polychrome mosaics of the late Roman period in Africa are among the finest that have come down to us. This example was found at Lambaesis in Algeria.

128. (below). **Vault mosaic from Santa Costanza.** 4th century AD. Santa Costanza in Rome was built as a mausoleum, probably in the time of Constantine the Great. The mosaics decorating the vault of the ambulatory combine

Christian and pagan subjects. In this detail *putti* are shown gathering grapes among the vine tendrils, treading the vintage and bringing in the grapes. These mosaics are the earliest surviving examples of the large-scale use of mosaic decoration on walls and vaulting in the Roman world.

the decorated mouldings. The classical simplicity and restraint of the Forum of Augustus later gave way to a much more elaborate style of decoration, which we think of as typically Roman, and which is exemplified by the Temple of the deified Vespasian, in the Forum.

The period of the Flavian Emperors saw a further ambitious programme of building in Rome; the erection of the Imperial Palace on the Palatine Hill, the construction of new baths, imperial fora, temples and other public buildings. The most famous monument of Flavian architecture is the Colosseum in Rome, the most massive of Roman amphitheatres, and one of the finest examples of Roman constructional technique (plate 113). Here is the characteristic Roman blend of Greek detail and Roman construction. The external walls of this immense building rise in four storeys of arches, decorated with engaged architecture of the Greek orders; on plan the oval of the auditorium, which is supported on massive concrete vaults, measures about 617 × 512 feet, and it is estimated that it would hold about 45,000 people. Theatres and amphitheatres constructed on these principles were put up everywhere during the first two centuries of the Empire; one of the finest and best preserved of the theatres is at Orange, in Provence, an area where the surviving Roman buildings are a striking memorial of the grandeur of the Roman Empire (see plate 115).

The Pantheon, built in the time of Hadrian, has long been one of the most admired of all Roman buildings; it has had a continuous history since classical antiquity, and is still in use as a Christian church. The great, circular, domed hall (figure 71) of the temple, lit by a circular opening at the top, encloses a space 142 feet in diameter and height; the walls were elaborately decorated with niches and coloured marble facings. In front of the rotunda is a colonnaded porch of six Corinthian columns supporting a pediment. By this time, the Romans had so perfected the techniques of building in concrete, that they were able to enclose enormous spaces with concrete vaults and domes, and they used the same methods in the construction of those vast complexes of buildings, which served the various purposes of the public bathing establishments. Throughout the Empire, they continued to give to their architecture the veneer of traditional Greek detail. The combination has given us the Roman triumphal arches, which were usually erected to commemorate military triumphs. They consist of an arched opening, or openings, flanked by engaged or detached columns, and surmounted by an entablature, above which is an attic usually serving as a base for a chariot group. Triumphal arches were erected from the late Republic to the late Empire (figure 91).

ROMAN PRIVATE TASTE UNDER THE EMPIRE

We have dwelt on the public monuments of the early Empire, because so much of what is characteristically Roman is to be found on them. But, in the long run, it was the private taste of the Romans that did most to keep alive the Greek tradition throughout the Empire. It was the whole-

67. **The Emperor Augustus.** 27 BC–AD 14. Marble. h. 6 ft. 7⅛ in. (2.01 m.). Vatican Museums. This statue was found in the Villa of Livia at Prima Porta near Rome. The reliefs on the breastplate represent the return, in 20 BC, of the Roman standards captured from Crassus at the Battle of Carrhae.

68. **Head of Vespasian.** AD 69–79. Marble. h. 1 ft. 4⅛ in. (41 cm.). British Museum, London. This portrait head of the Emperor Vespasian was found during excavations at Carthage in 1835–36.

69. **Claudius as Jupiter.** AD 41–54. Marble. h. 8 ft. 4 in. (2.54 m.). Vatican Museums. This statue of the Emperor Claudius as Jupiter, with eagle and oak-wreath, was found at Città Lavinia in 1865.

70. **Head of Trajan.** AD 98–117. Marble. h. 2 ft. 5¼ in. (74.5 cm.). British Museum, London. This portrait bust of the Emperor Trajan was found in the Roman Campagna in 1776.

71. **The Pantheon.** *c.* AD 126. Exterior view of the Pantheon in Rome, built early in the reign of Hadrian. A classical portico fronts the brick rotunda which was once faced with marble and stucco.

72. **The Pantheon. Interior view.** The decoration of the building, which has remained in continuous use since Roman times, has been much altered. A reconstructed section of the original marble facing may be seen in this view.

73. **Figure of Egypt.** *c.* AD 145. Marble. h. (of figure) 5 ft. (1.51 m.). Palazzo dei Conservatori, Rome. A personification of the province of Egypt, one of a series of province-figures from the Temple of the deified Hadrian, dedicated in AD 145.

hearted adoption of Greek art by the wealthy patricians of the late Republic that did most to Hellenise the Roman tradition, and, in the early Empire, there was no falling off in the taste for things Greek. The Romans continued to give employment to the copyists of Greek sculpture and painting. In sculpture the Roman period involved scarcely a single new figure-type, if we except new divinities in Greek guise (plate 105), and personifications of imperial ideas (figure 73). Only very rarely do we see aspects of a different taste, such as the increasing popularity of coloured marbles for statuary (plate 104). The private taste of the Romans of the Empire comes out best in the interiors of their private houses, which we know from Pompeii and Herculaneum. Copies of Greek sculpture and furniture in Greek style were used in gardens and rooms; Greek painting was the main inspiration of the interior decorators, who painted the frescoes on the walls. The epitome of philhellenic taste was to be found in the 'Villa', built by the Emperor Hadrian at Tivoli, near Rome. Here Hadrian laid out a great complex of buildings, many of them copied from, or inspired by, what he had seen during his travels in the provinces; he filled them with copies of Greek sculpture, paintings and mosaics. Though certainly the most philhellene of Emperors, he was no exception among Romans in his tastes.

ROMAN DECORATIVE PAINTING

We may consider here two aspects of Roman private taste: the painted interiors of their houses and the stone sarcophagi in which they were buried. Roman fresco-painting has already been mentioned for the light it throws upon the later history of Greek painting. We are not concerned here with the later schemes of Roman wall-decoration, except in so far as they illustrate the general lines of development of ancient painting, but something must be said about them in general terms. The earlier Second Style aimed at creating the illusion of space, whether with architectural vistas, landscape, or figure compositions, within the limits of a unified architectural scheme. In the later Second Style, which prevailed in the time of Augustus, the unity of the architecture was broken up by the introduction of large panel compositions, and, later on, the attempt at illusion was abandoned by many painters in favour of flat surfaces, with ornament based on architectural forms, but treated as arabesques, purely decorative in intention. Delicate columns and candelabra served to frame panel-compositions, which stood out against the brightly coloured flat background. Later still, in the so-called Fourth Style of Pompeii, there is compromise between flat decoration and architectural vista (plate 114), and throughout its later history, which, after AD 79, is poorly documented, Roman wall-decoration continued to make use of architectural elements or architectural divisions as the basis of its schemes. The pictures incorporated in the various Roman schemes of decoration continue to be closely inspired by the repertoire of Greek painting; the painters continued to paint epic scenes, land-

74. **Head of Mithras.** *c.* AD 200. Marble. h. 14½ in. (37 cm.). Guildhall Museum, London. Head of the god Mithras found in the excavation of the Walbrook Mithraeum, London, in 1954. It was made in Italy and imported into Britain.

75. **The Farnese Antinous.** Hadrianic
period. Marble. h. 6 ft. 6 in. (2 m.).
National Museum, Naples. Statue of
Antinous, the young Bithynian favourite
of the Emperor Hadrian. Antinous, who
was drowned in AD 130, is here represented as Hermes.

76. **Head of Hadrian.** AD 117–138.
Marble. h. 2 ft. 11½ in. (90 cm.): Palazzo
dei Conservatori, Rome. Hadrian was
the first Roman Emperor to wear a beard,
a feature which enhances the Greek
idealism of his portraits.

scapes, still life, scenes from everyday life, in the techniques
and styles invented by later Greek artists. It is very difficult
to say how much the Romans added to the repertoire. In
the time of Augustus there was a fashion for garden painting which gave the illusion of opening up the wall with a
view into a garden; a room in the Villa of Livia at Prima
Porta was completely decorated in this manner, and in a
style which contrives to give convincing effects of light and
atmosphere and vivid naturalistic detail (plate 108). The
big panel pictures are generally inspired by Greek models
of different periods with scenes from Greek mythology and
epic being especially popular. Pictures, such as the scene
illustrated in plate 111, which shows the rescue of Andromeda by Perseus, are probably adaptations of later Greek
masterpieces, and they show how the techniques of modelling in colour and of rendering light effects could now be
skilfully handled even by painters of moderate talent.

The Roman age had little to add to the development of
technique, but the appearance, in later Second-Style pictures, of what may be called an 'impressionistic' technique,
is something which has been claimed for the Romans. The
technique is used especially, and with especial success, in
the fantasy landscapes—views of imaginary countryside
with buildings, houses, harbour scenes. It abandons the
precise modelling of the Greek tradition in favour of colour

impressions, obtained with rapid strokes of the brush, by
which the painter can achieve powerful effects of light and
shade. One of the most striking examples of the use of this
technique is the picture illustrated in plate 109, which
shows the introduction, by night, of the Wooden Horse into
the city of Troy; a ghostly light pervades the whole picture,
and the slashing highlights on the foreground figures give
the scene a fine sense of drama. It is one of the most vivid
pieces of narration that has come down to us from the ancient world. The impressionistic technique appears first as
an experiment in the treatment of light and colour, not as
a deliberate reaction to 'classicism'. In the later Roman
Empire, however, when a more positive and widespread
reaction to the principles of pagan painting did exist, it
found a ready acceptance among artists, and became a
powerful influence in the development of painting.

ROMAN SARCOPHAGI

The early Roman sarcophagi illustrate, perhaps best of all,
the thoroughly Greek inspiration of the Roman decorative
arts. In the time of Hadrian the use of stone coffins for burial
became widespread among the wealthier classes in Rome,
and largely superseded the earlier practice of cremation,
where the ashes were placed in stone urns and funeral al-
tars. These sarcophagi were richly decorated with relief

77. **Neptune in his Chariot.** Late 2nd century AD. Mosaic. Baths of Neptune, Ostia. The mosaic, composed of black and white stones, shows Neptune being carried across the sea in a chariot drawn by sea-horses.

78. **The Melfi Sarcophagus.** Late 2nd century AD. Marble. h. 5 ft. 5 in. (1.65 m.). Melfi. Richly decorated column-sarcophagus made in Asia Minor and found at Melfi, in Italy. Figures of gods and heroes stand in the intercolumniations.

ornament, sometimes with purely decorative motifs, but most commonly with scenes taken from Greek mythology. The subjects are clearly based upon originals of Greek sculpture and painting, and the sarcophagi provide us with some of the liveliest and technically skilful sculpture that has come down to us from Roman times. The compositions, like those of the *Gigantomachy Sarcophagus*, in the Vatican, and the *Orestes Sarcophagus*, in the Lateran Museum, make up tapestries of figures in violent poses and movement that remind one of scenes on the Pergamene Altar. As the sarcophagi became taller, the complication of the groupings is increased, and the sculptors achieve remarkable feats in the massing of figures. The importance of the sarcophagi in the history of Roman art cannot be over-emphasised; not only did the production of them give permanent employment to sculptors in Italy, but the demand was so great and so widespread that workshops were soon set up in the eastern provinces of the Empire to satisfy it. Sarcophagi made in Asia Minor (figure 78), and Athens (figure 79), show the techniques and style of those centres, and in the 3rd century the sarcophagi became a principal source of knowledge for the history of Roman sculpture in general.

ROMAN ART IN THE PROVINCES AND BEYOND

In the first two centuries of the Empire, the Roman styles

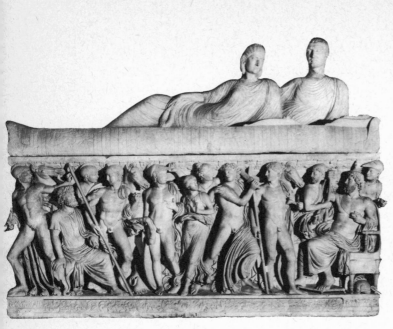

79. The Achilles Sarcophagus. 3rd century AD. Marble. h. 4 ft. 3½ in. (1.31 m.). Capitoline Museum, Rome. The reliefs depict the discovery of Achilles among the daughters of Lycomedes. Figures of the dead man and his wife recline on the lid. The sarcophagus was made in Greece.

80. Head of a Helvetian chief. 1st century AD. Bronze. h. 10¼ in. (26 cm.). Historical Museum, Berne. A portrait probably of a young prince of the Helvetii, modelled in a fine Roman style. The head comes from Prilly (Vaud).

of art and architecture spread to all the provinces, and their influence was felt beyond the frontiers. It is interesting to contrast the character of art in the Greek and eastern provinces, with that of the western provinces, which lacked the background of Hellenistic art. The Greek provinces, by providing artists trained in the techniques of Greek art, did most to keep alive the Greek tradition. In the west, the mixing of Greco-Roman with native traditions may produce a debased 'classicism', uncertain in proportion and ugly in detail or, where the local elements have a positive role to play, a genuinely fruitful union, as in the vigorous portrait of a Helvetian prince illustrated in figure 80, or in the well-known sculptured pediment from the Temple of Sulis-Minerva, at Bath (figure 82).

Beyond the eastern frontiers of the Empire, was the meeting place of classical and oriental art. The caravan cities of Dura Europos and Palmyra have provided us with sculptures and painting which, although they show strong Roman influence, are predominantly oriental in feeling (plate 121). Imported Roman works of art show their influence in Indian sculpture during the first centuries of the Empire (plate 120). The problem of provincial and foreign influences on the development of Roman art in general is an extremely complex one. The role of the eastern provinces, as creator of new techniques and transmitter of oriental ideas, is clear enough, but who can say to what extent the western provinces influence the progressive debasement of the classical tradition in the late Empire. But leaving aside these problems, the dominating impression of the art of the Roman Empire, as a whole, is of its uniformity. Everywhere in the days of its prosperity the Romanised provincials aspired to live like Romans, to adorn their houses with Roman sculpture, paintings and mosaics. The public monuments were built to standard patterns in all the principal towns. Even if, with the collapse of the Roman world, native traditions began to reassert themselves against classical representational art, the Roman influences went deep enough to have a place of importance in the future development of art in all the countries they touched.

THE DECLINE OF THE CLASSICAL TRADITION

The last part of this chapter is concerned with the decline of the Roman Empire, and of the classical tradition in art. There is, however, a danger of overstressing the aspect of decline, and failing to see the beginnings of a powerful new tradition inspired by new ideals which rejected the old. If we look at the art of Rome in the 3rd and 4th centuries AD solely in terms of the classical tradition, then we may see nothing but decline. We shall find painting and sculpture falling away from the standards set in the early Empire, we shall see the technical ability of the sculptors clearly inferior, we shall see painters losing the ability to handle line and colour in the old way. We may explain these in terms of the economic and political decline of the Roman Empire. We may even think that we have solved the problems of the decline of the classical tradition in art. But we shall be far

81. **Relief from Taxila, Punjab.** 2nd
century AD. (?). Stone. l. 15 in. (38 cm.).
The design of the frieze, showing garlands
of leaves supported by *putti* and with busts
in the loops, is basically classical but the
carving is the work of an Indian sculptor.

82. **The Bath Gorgon.** 2nd century AD.
Bath Stone. h. 8 ft. 2½ in. (2.50 m.).
Bath Museum, England. Central part
of the pedimental relief from the temple
of Sulis-Minerva at Bath. The central
feature is a carved shield decorated with
a head of a Gorgon and supported by
winged victories.

83. **Corinthian capital.** 1st century AD.
Stone. h. 3 ft. 3 in. (1.00 m.). Cirencester
Museum, England. Corinthian capital
decorated with busts on four sides found
at Cirencester. The wild Silenus-like
figure shown here probably represents
a Celtic fertility god.

from the truth if we fail to see that the rejection of much of what is essential in the classical tradition springs from a deliberate reaction to the ideals and aims of pagan culture. In fact, the causes of the breakdown of the classical tradition is one of the most complex problems in the whole history of ancient art. Our evidence comes mainly from an imperial tradition which tries hard to preserve the old values, and the elements of significant change are often hard to recognise. They manifest themselves in so many different ways; they may be differences of technique or they may be totally different methods of expression. We may find the picture confused from time to time by deliberate revivals of older styles, by seeing new ideas expressed in a symbolic language derived from pagan art. But one thing is certain, that from the time of the Antonines onwards, the old ideals of classical art failed to satisfy the aspirations of men, and this is the fundamental lesson of late Roman art.

LATE ROMAN ARCHITECTURE

Let us look first at the most obvious evidence of change in architecture, since here there is less obvious evidence of decline. It is true that the economic conditions of the late Empire produced periods when little public building was carried out, and the prosperity of the provincial cities was running down; but until the time of Constantine, when our survey ends, many very ambitious building projects were undertaken throughout the Roman world, especially under the Tetrarchy, and in the reign of Constantine himself.

Roman architecture had always been what has been called, 'a compromise between actual and apparent structure', that is, between Roman methods of building in concrete, and a decorative use of the classical orders. In the late Empire the Roman methods of building assert themselves even more strongly, and the use of the classical orders becomes more and more decorative and decadent; in some cases the latter are abandoned altogether. The buildings of the 3rd and 4th centuries AD, show increasingly ambitious planning of space and volume. The massive main hall of the Baths of Caracalla (figure P), measures 170 × 82 feet; its roof is carried on eight colossal piers, which supported the cross-vaulting. Arched openings between the piers gave access to side chambers, and other rooms of the Baths complex. The main hall of the Baths of Diocletian was even larger in scale. When, in AD 306, Maxentius designed a new administrative basilica near the Forum, he rejected the traditional columnar hall used in earlier basilicas, and adopted the design of the great halls of the Baths. The basilica had a nave built in three bays, each roofed with an intersecting barrel-vault, communicating side halls forming the aisles (plate 126).

Most of these late Roman buildings make extremely elaborate use of interior architectural decoration, but the use is rarely structural, and the detail becomes more and more unorthodox by classical standards. Architectural forms and styles of ornament developed in the eastern Roman provinces became more widespread. The carved fa-

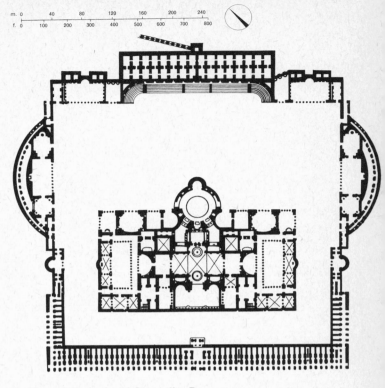

P. Plan of the baths of Caracalla, Rome.

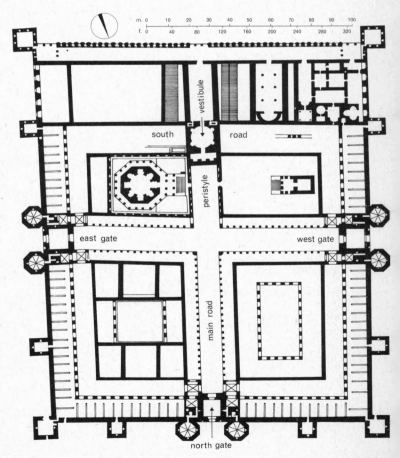

Q. Plan of Diocletian's Palace at Split.

84. **The Treasury at Petra.** *c.* 2nd century AD. h. 132 ft. (40 m.). Rock-cut tomb known as the 'Treasury', at Petra, in Jordan. Behind the elaborate architectural façade are several tomb-chambers.

çade of the so-called Treasury at Petra (figure 84), shows how daring some of the eastern versions of classical architecture were as early as the time of Hadrian; above a fairly orthodox colonnade we see a circular *aedicula*, flanked by curious half-pediments. The interiors of temples at Baalbek are sumptuously ornate, and show similar unorthodoxy of detail, and in the late Empire similar features begin to make a more obvious appearance in the west. We find arcades, with the arches springing directly off the columns, an arch interrupting a horizontal architrave, an arch within a pediment. The architectural ornament is carved to produce formal patterns with strong black-and-white effects, and shows very little connection with the classical motifs on which it is based.

Many of these new features in late Roman architecture illustrate the transition from the late Roman to the Byzantine style; they are decadent only in terms of the classical tradition. The late Roman styles of ornament, which we see so well, for example, in Diocletian's Palace at Split (plate 123), lead naturally to the Byzantine. The latest Roman experiments in the construction of dome and vault, and the discovery of the spherical pendentive, making possible the transition from vertical wall to domed roof, were to make possible such masterpieces as Santa Sophia. The brick arched exterior of the Basilica of Trier, which gains its effect

without any resort to classical decoration, has the promise of a totally different approach to architectural design. Late Roman architecture almost everywhere provides such evidence of creative change. A contrast is provided by a number of buildings which attempt to prolong the classical tradition, and in these the evidence of decline seems to dominate. The classic example is provided by the Arch of Constantine, put up by that Emperor in AD 312, to commemorate his victories. It is undeniably a most successful building, perhaps the finest of Roman triumphal arches, but its success is achieved by recourse to methods which imply a sense of inferiority. Most of the architectural detail and much of the sculpture, is taken from earlier buildings; the contemporary sculpture, when it attempts to imitate the old, is far inferior in technique and totally different in style. The Arch of Constantine illustrates the decline of classical form, and was indeed taken as the object lesson of this theme by Bernard Berenson. But the Arch of Constantine illustrates only one aspect of late-Roman architecture and probably its least significant.

NEW TRENDS IN RELIEF-SCULPTURE

It is more difficult to recognise the new trends in sculpture and painting than in architecture, because they manifest themselves in many different ways on established traditions. The commemorative sculpture of the early Antonine

85. **Panel from the Arch of Septimius
Severus,** Rome. AD 203. Marble. The
panel illustrates events in the Emperor's
eastern campaigns.

period is still firmly founded on the classical tradition, but,
in the time of Marcus Aurelius, the signs of change are already clear. The contrast between the reliefs on the Column
of Trajan, and those on the column erected to commemorate the victories of Marcus Aurelius at the end of the 2nd
century, brings them clearly before us. The design of the
later column is based on the earlier, but the differences in
style and technique are very marked. Most obvious of all,
perhaps, is the decline in the modelling of the human figure and in the carving of drapery where black and white
effects replace the rounded forms of the classical tradition.
There is uncertainty in proportions, and the sculptor tends
to concentrate his attention on the head at the expense of
the body. He makes much more effort to express feelings, to
portray the sufferings of war instead of giving a cold factual
record of events. He tries to involve us in events, and to do
this he abandons many of the stock conventions of the
Greco-Roman tradition. He tends to reject the traditional
profile view of a scene, and turns the figures to face the
spectator, almost as though they were posing for him; this
tendency towards frontality becomes more and more
marked in late Roman sculpture, until in the long frieze of
the Arch of Constantine it has assumed the authority of a
law. The decline of classical form, in favour of a more expressive style, is accompanied by an abandonment of any

attempt to create an illusion of reality and depth, by means
of subtle carving on many planes. The conventions become
more naive and, because more naive, also more direct. Two
rows of figures, one behind the other, are simply shown one
above the other, the background figures appearing in the
form of a series of heads (figure 92). A bird's eye perspective is
sometimes used to give the setting for action (figure 85). The
interpretation of these new elements of technique, design,
and expression is not always clear. Some appear as a deliberate reaction to classicism, some seem to express uncon-
sciously new aims and notions. But all of them show un-
equivocally a new approach to the problems of representational art, and an increasing tendency to reject the old.

THE LATER SARCOPHAGI

The later Roman sarcophagi provide a clear record of the
changing attitudes of mind in the late Roman Empire. As
we have seen, classical themes carved in the classical manner satisfied the taste of the Roman upper class in Hadrian's
reign; in the Antonine period specifically Roman themes
became more common. A fine series of Battle sarcophagi
begins at this time, and there are sarcophagi with scenes
from Roman military and civil life. But mythological scenes
continue to predominate; Bacchanalian subjects were especially popular. The demand for these sarcophagi was

86. **A Triumphal Procession.** *c.* AD 200.
Marble. h. 5 ft. 7 in. (1.70 m.). Lepcis
Magna. Part of the triumphal procession
of Septimius Severus on a panel from the
Arch of Septimius at Lepcis in Tripoli-
tania. The Emperor stands in his chariot
with his sons Caracalla and Geta.

87. **The Ludovisi Battle Sarcophagus.**
c. AD 250. Marble. h. 5 ft. (1.53 m.).
Museo delle Terme, Rome. Battle between Romans and barbarians, probably
Dacians. The figure of the dead man,
a Roman general, dominates the scene.

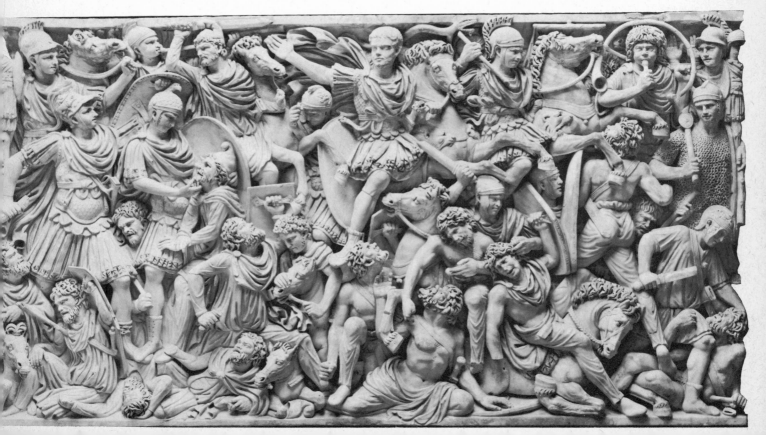

88. **A Christian sarcophagus.** Constantinian period. Marble. Lateran Museum, Rome. The sarcophagus is decorated with scenes from the Old and New Testaments. The central roundel encloses half-figures of the dead man and his wife; the heads were never finished.

met by workshops all over the Roman world; some of the finest and most elaborate were produced in Asia Minor (figure 78) and in Greece (figure 79). The Asiatic sarcophagi show the typically eastern style of carving ornament, with deep cutting and strong black and white effects; those of Greece try to preserve the classical figure-styles and classical techniques of modelling. In the Roman workshops of the 3rd century, ugly faces and ill-proportioned bodies became more common. In contrast with the cool classicism of the *Achilles Sarcophagus* (figure 79), from Greece, a contemporary sarcophagus in Rome shows less attention to the forms of the body and concentrates the interest in the faces which are often disproportionately large.

The symbolism, too, is different. The popular lion-hunt theme symbolises the triumph of life over death; other themes express the ideals of virtue, bravery, of philosophic contemplation of the after-life, to which the thoughts of the Romans in the troubled times of the late Empire were increasingly turning. One of the most magnificent of all Roman sarcophagi is the Ludovisi *Battle Sarcophagus* of about 250 AD; the battle theme is a traditional one but the whole conception is utterly different from the cold impersonal battle scenes of the earlier period. Here the struggles and sufferings of the barbarians seem to symbolise the struggles of life, and the triumphant gesture of the general suggests

his escape from earthly sufferings to a better life (figure 87).

Some Christian themes begin to take their place on the sarcophagi; the sarcophagus of the Constantinian period, now in the Lateran Museum (figure 88), with scenes from the Old and New Testaments arranged in two tiers, cultivates a deliberate ugliness in the figure style, which seems a complete negation of classical ideals. In this particular example, anti-classical feeling is very strong, much stronger than in many other works of the period, but it serves well to bring to our notice the fact that we have to do not simply with decline, but with a definite reaction to all the pagan values of the classical world. Ugliness is deliberately cultivated to show how far man has fallen from God's image. If we were to follow Christian sculpture further, we should find that it begins to compromise with classical art and to draw fresh inspiration from pagan themes. There is Greek beauty in the 4th-century figure of Christ (figure 89), a reminder that the classical tradition is not dead, but could be transformed to express the new ideals of the age.

PORTRAITS OF THE LATE EMPIRE

The portraits of the late Empire change the whole conception of portraiture. As we have seen, the combination of Greek and Roman taste and techniques gave early Roman portraiture the same fundamental characteristics as that of

90. **Head of Trajan Decius.** *c.* AD 250.
Marble. h. 13 in. (33 cm.). Capitoline
Museum, Rome. Portrait of an Emperor
who reigned briefly from AD 249–51 and
died fighting against the Goths.

89. **Christ.** 4th century AD. Marble.
h. 2 ft. 4 in. (71 cm.). Museo delle Terme,
Rome. This statuette is believed to represent Christ, youthful and beardless,
as he was first portrayed in ancient times.

the Hellenistic world. The Greco-Roman portrait is a careful record of a man's features, plastically modelled, and attempting to express his personality and character; one emperor may prefer the cold, remote expression of the face,
another the intensity of a momentary glance, but none of
the portraits give away the subject's feelings, aspirations,
and sufferings. The man is kept at a distance. This conception of the portrait lasts until the time of the Antonines;
thereafter, striking changes begin to take place. The portraits of 3rd-century emperors and private persons try to
penetrate the very soul of the man. The artist concentrates
on the essentials of expression; he may pay little attention
to the details of the hair and beard, but devote immense
care to the expression of the eyes, the lines of the face, the
set of the mouth. One of the finest of these 3rd-century portraits is the head of Trajan Decius, carved about AD 250
(figure 90); in it we seem to see not only the struggles and
perplexities of the man, but of the whole age in which he
lived. He seems to symbolise an age. These powerful forms
of expression, which bring these men of the 3rd century so
much nearer to our understanding, can also be used to
make them more remote from us. Once the artists, in order
to get beyond a man's features, begin to remodel and even
distort them, the way is open for the kind of symbolic rendering of the human face which we associate with the art of

Byzantium. We see it already in the colossal head of the Emperor Constantine broken from the statue which once stood in the Basilica of Constantine; this is no portrait, but an impersonal, symbolic image of imperial majesty, which has drawn the man away from us into the realm of the superhuman and divine.

CATACOMB PAINTINGS

After we lose the guiding thread of Pompeian painting, the history of Roman painting is hard to follow. Much of what has come down to us is second-rate. The paintings from the catacombs, which begin in the 3rd century AD, provide a body of painting with a completely new source of inspiration, but much of the work is at a very poor level of craftsmanship and technique. The mosaics become increasingly important as a source of understanding the new trends in representational art; wall mosaic increases in popularity, heralding its supremacy in the decorative art of the Byzantine period (plate 128). The general tendencies in late Roman painting and decoration are clear enough. As in sculpture, the painters lose interest in the problems of representing space and of modelling in colour; they show a preference for frontal figures, painted against flat backgrounds in a sketchily impressionistic style, opposed to the modelling of classical painting. Sometimes this impressionistic style is combined with hard outline drawing, which gives the figures a rigidity and conventionalism which has a very Byzantine look. Though they lose in subtlety, these pictures gain in directness and simplicity of representation, and, by the time of Constantine, we get pictures, like the Christ in Majesty from the catacomb of Domitilla, that give us a completely new vision of art. The splendours of Byzantine mosaic are heralded in the rich use of colour, to be seen in the mosaics of Santa Costanza, probably the Mausoleum of Constantina, daughter of Constantine the Great, who died in 354 (plate 128). The subjects are traditional pagan themes, but handled with a freshness and brightness which few pagan mosaics can equal.

PAGAN AND CHRISTIAN ART

The last section of this chapter is inevitably inconclusive. The great achievements of early Christian art belong to a period outside the scope of this book. Here we see only the beginnings of a new tradition, working uncertainly on an old tradition, that of the classical world. The early Christians were frightened of pagan art, in much the same way that Roman patricians of the old school in the last century of the Republic had been frightened of Hellenistic art. In the end, both the Romans and the early Christians had to compromise, but the early Christians rejected the ideals of classical culture, and introduced fundamentally different sources of inspiration, so changing the whole character and purpose of art. But if we follow the history of art beyond its late Roman phase, we shall find many examples where the classical spirit and classical techniques live on, until their triumphant revival at the Renaissance.

91. **The Arch of Constantine.** AD 312. This arch was erected in Rome to commemorate the Emperor's victories. The sculpture with which it is decorated was largely taken from earlier buildings, but the long, narrow panels (see figure 92) are contemporary work.

92. **The Emperor Constantine on the Rostra.** This relief from the north side of the Arch of Constantine shows the Emperor addressing the people from the Rostra in the Roman forum. The Rostra are flanked by seated statues of past Emperors.

Glossary

Aeolic. A type of capital with scrolls, found in Asia Minor and Etruria; sometimes thought of as an early form of Ionic.

Agora. Greek market place, where people assembled and public business was performed.

Amphora. A two-handled jar, especially for wine.

Anthropoid. In the form of a human being (Greek, anthropos = man).

Apse. In classical architecture this can be both a semi-circular recess in a wall, or that part of a building that is semi-circular in plan, for example the east end of a basilica.

Archaic. Used to describe the period of Greek Art between about 700 and 480 BC.

Ashlar. A type of masonry, using large regularly shaped blocks laid in courses.

Atrium. Central space of a Roman house, round which the rooms are grouped. It was lit by an opening in the roof.

Basilica. Large oblong hall, usually divided into nave and aisles by columns.

Black-figure. A style of Greek vase-painting, in which the figures are painted in black silhouette on the red ground of the fired clay (see plate 37).

Bucchero. Italian word for a type of fine grey or black pottery, especially found in Etruria.

Canopic jar. Vase with the body of rudimentary human form, and the lid in the form of a head; called after a type used in Egypt.

Caryatid. Female figure taking the place of a column in a classical building.

Cella. The main chamber of a Greek temple.

Chiton. A Greek garment of light material with sleeves (see plate 33).

Chryselephantine. Of gold and ivory; these materials were used especially for large cult-statues in the Greek world.

Cista. A cylindrical or rectangular box.

Classical. In the title of this book the word is used in the sense of Greek and Roman. In other books it is sometimes used to describe the period of Greek art between 480 BC and 323 BC, and in its most restricted sense, the period between 450 and 400 BC.

Composite. A type of Roman capital combining elements of Ionic and Corinthian (see page 134).

Cornice. The uppermost projecting member of an entablature (see page 38).

Crater. A large mixing bowl.

Cycladic. Used to describe the Bronze Age cultures of the Aegean islands (Cyclades).

Cyclopean. A type of masonry, making use of rough hewn stones of large size. Literally, made by the Cyclops, a race of giants.

Daedalic. From Daedalus, the mythical first sculptor of Greece, used to describe the stone sculpture of the 7th century BC.

Dipylon. A cemetery in Athens, which has been excavated in recent years. 'Dipylon' vases are the big Attic geometric vases of the later 8th century, decorated with figure scenes (see plate 23).

Doric order. See page 38 and fig. C, where the names of the various parts are given.

Exedra. An open recess or alcove, either semi-circular or rectangular in plan. Niche or small apse.

Fibula. Clasp or buckle, rather like a safety pin.

Fresco. Painting on plaster, the paint being applied when the plaster is still wet.

Granulation. A goldsmith's technique of decoration, using small granules of gold.

Helladic. The Bronze Age cultures of mainland Greece. The late Helladic period is known as the Mycenaean period.

Hellenistic. The period between 323 BC, the death of Alexander the Great, and 31 BC.

Herm. Pillar surmounted by a human head: the genitals are usually carved on the pillar. A short herm form was much used for portrait heads in Roman times.

Himation. A mantle of heavy material worn by men and women.

Ionia. The western coast of Asia Minor, colonised by the Greeks.

Ionic order. See page 75 and fig. H.

Kore. A young girl; generic term for the standing female figures of the archaic period.

Kouros. A young man; generic term for the standing male statues of the archaic period.

Lekythos. A Greek vase used for oil and perfume. One of the commonest forms, used especially for funeral dedications is illustrated on plate 53.

Linear B. A syllabic script, used to write an early form of Greek in Crete and Greece between 1400 and 1200 BC. Linear A is the earlier Cretan syllabic script, as yet undeciphered.

Meander. Greek key-pattern.

Megaron. Bronze Age house with porch and main chamber having a central hearth (see page 33).

Metope. See Doric order.

Minoan. The Bronze Age in Crete, so called after the legendary King Minos.

Neo-Attics. School of sculptors active in Athens in 1st century BC and 1st century AD, making copies and adaptations of earlier Greek sculpture for the Roman Market.

Niello. A black alloy of copper and silver used for inlaying on metal.

Orientalising. Used to describe the period of oriental influences in Greek Art, especially the 7th century BC (see page 36).

Pediment. The gable of a Greek or Roman building; the word *tympanum* is used for the area enclosed between the cornices.

Pendentive. A constructional form used to rest a dome on an internally square structure.

Peplos. A sleeveless garment of heavy material worn by women (see plate 33).

Peristyle. A colonnade round a temple building or inside a courtyard or room.

Pilaster. A flat pillar engaged against a wall.

Podium. A base, used especially of the base on which Roman temples stand.

Propylaea. A monumental entrance to an architectural complex (see plate 49).

Proto-. As in proto-geometric and proto-attic, the prefix is used to describe an early stage of a particular style.

Red-figure. A style of Greek vase-painting in which the figures appear in the natural red of the fired clay and the background is painted black (see page 57).

Repoussé. Technique of producing relief-work on metal objects.

Rhyton. Vessel in the form of a horn or animal head, with a hole in the bottom, to which the lips were placed for drinking.

Sarcophagus. A coffin.

Sauceboat. A vessel, somewhat resembling a modern sauceboat, common in the early Helladic period in Greece.

Stele. A gravestone, often in the form of a tall flat pillar.

Stoa. A colonnaded walk, usually with a blank rear wall.

Terracotta. Fired clay; used especially for figures made by this method.

Tholos. A circular structure; the word is applied to the Mycenaen chamber tombs (see fig. 5).

Tuscan order. See page 130.

Villanovan. The pre-Etruscan Iron Age culture in Etruria and the Bolognese.

Voussoirs. The wedge shaped blocks that form an arch. The central stone is called the 'key stone'.

White ground. A technique of Attic vase-painting, in which figures are drawn or painted on a white coating put over the surface of the vase.

Further Reading List

The Greek Bronze Age

Graham, J. W., The Palaces of Crete, 1962
Hutchinson, R. W., Prehistoric Crete, 1962
Marinatos, S. and Hirmer, M., Crete and Mycenae, 1960
Matz, F., Crete and Early Greece, 1962
Taylour, Lord William, The Myceneans, 1964

Greek Art and Archaeology

Beazley, J. D. and Ashmole, B., Greek Sculpture and
    Painting, 1932
Boardman, J., The Greeks Overseas, 1964
Cook, J. M., The Greeks in Ionia and the East, 1962
MacKendrick, P., The Greek Stones Speak, 1963
Richter, G. M. A., A Handbook of Greek Art, 1959
—, Archaic Greek Art, 1949
Woodhead, A. G., The Greeks in the West, 1962
Zschietzschmann, W., Hellas and Rome, The Classical
    World in Pictures, 1959

Greek Sculpture

Bieber, M., The Sculpture of the Hellenistic Age, 1955
Lullies, R., and Hirmer, M., Greek Sculpture, 1957
Richter, G. M. A., The Sculpture and Sculptors of the
    Greeks, 1950
Stuart Jones, H., Ancient Writers on Greek Sculpture, 1895

Greek Painting and Pottery

Arias, P. E., and Hirmer, M., A History of Greek Vase
    Painting, 1962
Cook, R. M., Greek Painted Pottery, 1960
Devambez, P., Greek Painting, 1962
Lane, A., Greek Pottery, 1947
Robertson, M., Greek Painting, 1953
Swindler, M. H., Ancient Painting, 1929

Greek Architecture

Dinsmoor, W. B., The Architecture of Ancient Greece, 3rd
    ed., 1950
Lawrence, A. W., Greek Architecture, 1957
Robertson, D. S., A Handbook of Greek and Roman
    Architecture, 1943
Wycherley, R. E., How the Greeks Built Cities, 2nd ed.,
    1962

Etruscan Art

Bloch, R., The Etruscans, 1960
Dennis, G., The Cities and Cemeteries of Etruria, 2 vols,
    1878
Pallottino, M., The Etruscans, 1955
—, Art of the Etruscans, 1955
—, Etruscan Painting, 1953
Riis, P. J., An Introduction to Etruscan Art, 1953

Roman Art and Architecture

Berenson, B., The Arch of Constantine, 1954
Charleston, R. J., Roman Pottery, 1955
Kähler, H., Rome and her Empire, 1963
Maiuri, A., Roman Painting, 1953
Richter, G. M. A., Ancient Italy, 1955
Stenico, A., Roman and Etruscan Painting, 1963
Strong, E. (Mrs. Arthur), Roman Sculpture, 1911 (super-
    seded by the Italian edition, La Scultura Romana,
    1927)
Strong, D. E., Roman Imperial Sculpture, 1961
Toynbee, J. M. C., Art in Roman Britain, 1962
Wheeler, Sir M., Roman Art and Architecture, 1964

Acknowledgements

Line drawings in this volume were based on illustrations in the publications listed below. Paul Hamlyn Ltd gratefully acknowledge the consent of the publishers.

A and B   S. Marinatos and M. Hirmer: *Crete and Mycenae*. Thames and Hudson, London
C   A. Boetticher: *Olympia, Das Fest und seine Stätte*. Verlagsbuchhandlung Julius Springer, Berlin
D and I   W. B. Dinsmoor: *The Architecture of Ancient Greece*. B. T. Batsford, London
E and F   R. Lullies and M. Hirmer: *Greek Sculpture*. Thames and Hudson, London
H   Th. Wiegand-H. Schrader: *Priene*. Stiftung Preussischer Kulturbesitz
K   Fasolo and Gullini: *Il Santuario della Fortuna Primigenia a Palestrina*. Istituto di archeologia, Università di Roma
N, O and Q   H. Kähler: *Rome and Her Empire*. Holle Verlag, Baden Baden
P   A. H. Middleton: *Remains of Ancient Rome*. A. and C. Black, London

Photographs were supplied by the following:

Colour: Joachim Blauel 27, 43, 44, Boston Museum of Fine Arts 29, The British Museum Photographic Service 45, 121, Giraudon 42, 116, Paul Hamlyn Photographic Archives 47, 91, 125, Fritz Henle 11, 38, 64, 70, Hans Hinz 2, 48, 58, 80, 81, Hirmer Verlag 15, 16, 17, 77, Michael Holford 22, 25, 37, 52, 53, 55, 57, 72, 87, 90, 93, 94, 100, 105, 108, 112, 117, 119, 122, 124, 126, 128, Hughes-Gilbey 1, 3, 4, 5, 6, 7, 8, 9, 10, 12, 13, 14, 18, 19, 20, 21, 23, 26, 28, 30, 31, 32, 33, 34, 35, 36, 39, 40, 46, 51, 54, 56, 59, 60, 61, 62, 63, 65, 66, 68, 69, 73, 74, 75, 76, 78, 79, 84, 85, 92, 102, 104, 106, 107, 109, 110, 111, 114, 118, 120. A. F. Kersting 49, 113, Metropolitan Museum of Art, New York 24, Paul Popper 115, Presses Universitaires de France 41, Oscar Savio 83, Scala 82, 86, 98, 99, 101, Rev. Schoder S.J. 127, V. Serventy 50, Skira 67, Staatliche Museum, E. Berlin 71, Viewpoint Projects 123, Roger Viollet 103, Joseph Ziolo/André Held 88, 89, 95, 96, 97.

Black and white: Acropolis Museum, Athens 16, Alinari 13, 24, 29, 48, 58, 60, 64, 65, 71, 87, 91, Anderson/Alinari 44, 75, 88, 92, Archaeological Survey of India 82, Bath Museum, 81, Berne Historical Museum 80, Bologna Archaeological Museum 25, Boudot-Lamotte 10, The British Museum Photographic Service 22, 43, 52, 54, 56, 57, 59, 68, 70, J. Allan Cash 20, 26, Danish National Museum 63, R. Descharnes 12, Dresden Kunstsammlungen 31, Fototeca Unione 85, Fox Photos 19, German Archaeological Institute, Athens 8, 11, 15, 17, German Archaeological Institute, Rome 73, 78, 86, Hirmer 5, 18, 27, 30, 32, 49, 50, 55, Michael Holford 1, 6, 33, 36, 38, 40, 53, 72, 76, 79, 89, 90, Hughes-Gilbey 4, 7, 9, 21, 23, 34, 37, 47, Larousse 28, Madrid Archaeological Museum 51, Mansell 2, 46, Photo Marburg 62, Middle East Airlines 84, Ny Carlsberg Glyptotek 45, 61, Schneider-Lengyel 14, Toni Schneiders 3, Warburg Institute 74, 83, Vatican City Photographic Archives 35, 42, 67, 69, Viewpoint Projects 39, 41, 66, 77.

EVENTS	ART AND ARCHITECTURE

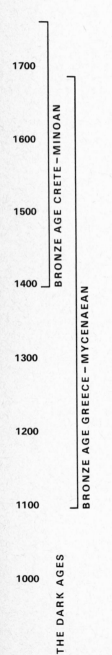

2000   *Arrival of Greeks in Greece*
     Minoan Palaces built

1900

1800

                                          Polychrome pottery
                                          Kamares ware

1700   *Palaces destroyed and rebuilt*

     Transition from hieroglyphic to Linear 'A' script

1600   *Cretan fresco painting · Naturalism in the Arts*

     1570-1500 Mycenaean shaft graves

1500   *Marine' style*

     Linear 'B' script

                                        Palace' style

1400   *Destruction of Knossos*
     Mycenaean Supremacy

                                 Hagia Triada Sarcophagus
     Lion Gate · Treasury of Atreus

1300

1200   *Trojan War (?)*   *Warrior vase*
     Collapse of Mycenaean World

     Beginning of the Iron Age
                                        Sub-Mycenaean pottery
     Dorian invasions of Greece

1100

1000   *Ionian migration*   *Proto-geometric pottery*

(Vertical labels at left:) BRONZE AGE CRETE–MINOAN · BRONZE AGE GREECE–MYCENAEAN · THE DARK AGES

THE ARCHAIC PERIOD

THE CITY STATES

DECLINE OF CITY STATES
RISE OF MACEDON
THE RISE OF ROME   **THE H**

POTTERY

c.850-700 Geometric pottery

525-400 Attic red-figure pottery
Andokides painter
Euthymides
725-625 Proto-Corinthian pottery   Euphronios
700-625 Proto-Attic pottery   Kleophrades painter
Other 'orientalising' wares   Caeretan hydriae   450-c.400 White ground lekythoi
625-500 Attic black-figure pottery   Meidias painter
Big Dipylon vases   Exekias   Berlin painter   Decline of painted pottery
Nessos painter   Oltos   Achilles painter   End of red-figure vases

PAINTING & MOSAICS

c.470 Polygnotus 'first great painter'
c.440 Parrhasius, and c.420 Zeuxis, painters in Ath
c.430 Apollodorus introduced shading and colo
c.330 Apelles, Court pa
Original of Alexand
Painted metopes of Thermon   c.300 Pebble m.
Archaic Etruscan tomb paintings   Trium

SCULPTURE

c.450 Myron's Discobolus
456-430 Polycleitos' athletic sculptures
c.450 Pheidias' Lemnian Athena
The Mantiklos Apollo   c.438 Pheidias' Athena Parthenos
Geometric small bronzes and terracottas   c.640 Kore of Auxerre   c.400 Stele of Hegeso
c.650 Earliest monumental sculpture   fl. c.360 Scopas
Daedalic style   c.530 Anavyssos kouros   c.340 Praxiteles' Hermes
c.530 Peplos kore   Lysippus' Apoxyomenos
c.600 Sunion kouros   c.480 Kritian boy   Development of Portraite
Bronze group of Herakles and Nessos   Apollo of Veii   317 Last Attic grav

ARCHITECTURE

c.525 Siphnian Treasury at Delphi
c.490 Temple of Aphaia at Aegina
474-456 Temple of Zeus at Olympia
450-440 Temple of Hephaestos
Temple of Hera at Samos (First peripteral temple)   c.350 Mausoleum at Halicar
447-432 Parthenon   c.325 Temple of Diana
421-409 Erechtheum
Doric order evolved   437-432 Propylaea
c.600 Temple of Hera at Olympia   c.350 Theatre of Epidaurus
Temple of Artemis at Corcyra   Town plan of Priene

LITERATURE

c.530 Pythagoras, philosopher and mathematician
585 Thales forecast total eclipse of the sun   d.270 Ep
Beginning of Philosophy
Lyric poetry of Alcaeus and Sappho
Homeric poems composed   534 Thespis staged first drama at Athens
Hesiod's 'Works and Days'   429-347 Plato wrote Socratic dialogues
Greek alphabet introduced   526-455 Aeschylus wrote oldest surviving tragedies
Odes of Pindar   384-322 Aristotle, philosopher and
498-406 Sophocles. His tragedies include Antigone, Oedipus
480-428 Herodotus. 'The Father of History'
Thucydides, wrote History of the Peloponnesian Wa
384-322 Demosthenes, Attic orato
343-292 Menander, write
430-359 Xenophon. The Anabasis   c.
450-385 Aristophanes, writer of Old Comedy
25
470-407 Euripides. Eighteen of his plays survive
c.546 Anaximander wrote first known prose work
312 Theocritus v
469-399 Socrates taught in Athens
c.460 Hippocrates, 'The Father of Medicine'
436-338 Isocrates orator and teacher at Athens
400-325 Diogenes the Cynic
287-212 Ar
c.300 Euclid com
fl.302 Zeno foun

HISTORY

776 First Olympic Games held   Rome under Etruscan rule   443-431 Pericles supreme in Athens   261-
c.750 Colonisation of Cumae   546-528 Pisistratus, tyrant of Athens   336-330 Alexander def
Rich Etruscan tombs at Caere, Praeneste   479-432 Athenian Empire   ✕333 Battle   273 Colo
753 Foundation of Rome   and elsewhere   546 Croesus of Lydia defeated by Cyrus of Persia   of the Issus   281 Pyrrh
753-510 Traditional Rule of the Seven kings of Rome   499 Ionian revolt and Persian invasions 490 & 480
850-700 Villanovan culture in Etruria and Bolognese   ✕480 Battle   396 Capture of Veii by Romans
of Salamis   Decline of city states and rise of Maced
✕490 Battle of Marathon   346 Philip of Macedon ga
c.592 Solon's reforms at Athens   431-404 Peloponnesian War   281 Fall of
535 Sea battle of Alalia   390 Sack of Rome by Gauls
c.500 Height of Etruscan power, expansion into Po valley
509 Rome expelled the kings
L. Junius Brutus first consul
474 Etruscan defeat at Battle of Cumae